A PICTURE *of* GOD

Barry Bailey

A PICTURE OF GOD

ABINGDON PRESS
Nashville

A PICTURE OF GOD

Copyright © 1991 by Abingdon Press

This book is printed on recycled acid-free paper.

Library of Congress Cataloging-in-Publication Data

BAILEY, BARRY, 1926-
A picture of God / Barry Bailey.
p.   cm.
ISBN 0-687-31019-9 (alk. paper)
1. God—Biblical teaching. I. Title.
BS544.B35   1991
231—dc20   90-26686

MANUFACTURED IN THE UNITES STATES OF AMERICA

*F*or
the joy and support that they bring me, this book is dedicated to my wife, Joan, who has assisted me in every good thing I have tried to do; our daughter, Janice Robinson; her husband, Dr. Roger Robinson; their children, Wesley Lamar and Laura Allison; our son, Barry Kessler Bailey; my mother, Marguerite Bailey; and to my sister and brother-in-law, Tommye and Dub Wells, and their family.

ACKNOWLEDGMENTS

My great appreciation goes to Gail Cooke, who has edited this book along with the six others. If she doesn't edit, I don't write. I am also grateful to Eugenia Hinds, my secretary, who transcribes my sermons week after week.

In addition, I am deeply appreciative of the ministers of First United Methodist Church, with whom I have the privilege of working, Dr. Jake Shelley, the Rev. Weldon Haynes, Dr. William Longsworth, the Rev. Larry Grubb, the Rev. Kay Johnson, the Rev. Barbara Wordinger, Dr. C. C. Sessions, and all of the staff, who do such a superb job of serving literally thousands of people every week.

My appreciation is also extended to the congregation of First United Methodist Church, Fort Worth,

Texas, and to all those who worship with us by way of television. Other than writing for myself, I suppose what I do is try to write something that is meaningful to them. For their creative influence, I am most grateful.

CONTENTS

1

A Picture of God

*H*ave you ever thought of God suffering? The three basic ideas that we are classically taught about God are his omnipotence, his omniscience, and his omnipresence. These sound good, and there are times when we want our God to be all-powerful, all-knowing, and everywhere at one time. These ideas about God are true to some extent, but, like all truth, there is also another side.

I believe that God is omnipresent; God is everywhere at one time. As far as God's being omniscient, God does not have everything worked out. If he does, then everything is a farce. If God has the script and we are on stage just playing the parts, you wonder what kind of a dull, rainy afternoon God had when he planned things of this nature. That would be demonic. Just the opposite is true. God is in the struggle; God has a purpose. God has a direction in which he would want us to go, much as a good teacher has a direction for his or her students or a composer has a direction or a parent working with a child has a direction he or she hopes the child will go in. Good parents do not want to dominate, control, or superimpose themselves on their children. That would destroy the child. A parent works more as a catalyst, working from within the person as much as possible.

The fact that God is in the struggle is repeatedly shown by Jesus in his actions. I would imagine there was not a great deal of fun involved in being Jesus. We would be destroyed if we were to live the life he lived. From the post-resurrection perspective, we can talk about how great it must have been to be Jesus. Yet, if we really look at his life, we see that it was quite obviously something else.

So it was in Jesus' life repeatedly, and so it must be in the mind of God. Jesus shows us God. It is not that God cries all the time or is exhausted in the struggle. It is being the catalyst, trying to bring into existence what ought to be. It is the tempting idea; it is the tip of the iceberg, which indicates the possible depth. It is the birth of a baby when you love the child that is, yet occasionally catch a fleeting glimpse of the child that might be. It is the way you experience your own feelings once in a while, when you are aware of the possibility of some change in your life and the direction that you might go in, knowing that this change is a much healthier approach.

God is not all-powerful in that God superimposes his will upon us so everything that happens is his will. At times, when I look at life, I feel that most of the things that happen are not the will of God. The terrible things that occur in the world, by and large, are the results of what we do to one another. We need to pray to have in us the mind that was in Christ so that we will not do these things to each other. Jesus struggled, trying to show us God. He tried to show us the wrongs that we do to each other. He attempted to change us by helping us fall in love with life and the basic things that matter, such as compassion and mercy.

Yet, instead of seeing God as creative, a God who is a catalyst, we see a God who created the whole world, a world peopled by sinners, and God has turned his back and punished us ever since. We see God as all-powerful, being able to end the world whenever he wants and to do anything else he pleases. That would be true only if God were a demon possessing power. But God is not demonic, and God does not have all power. God has all-presence, and the presence is his power. His power is consistent with his character. Jesus' power was consistent with his character, and his character happened to be love. Therefore, his power could not be unleashed like the power of a Hitler or a Napoleon. Yet, we see God as being all-powerful and, in a sense, expect God to use his power in much the same way a dictator or a tyrant wields power, destroying those who oppose as they wished. Hence, we reason that David can destroy Goliath because God is God and David is on God's side.

Jesus taught the opposite. Jesus did not even try to destroy the people who were crucifying him. He knew the way to destroy an enemy is to make the person a friend; kindness and love are the ways to destroy evil. It is done with insight.

13

God continues to struggle, working to make things better more than we do. The evil in the world is not a punishment of God. By and large, it is the sum total of what we do to each other, with the exception of storms or natural disasters. And those events are certainly not the will of God; they are acts of nature. God is not controlling nature by making a storm rage in one place and the sun shine in another. God gives us the capacity to appreciate good weather when it comes and to endure suffering when it comes. God is that within us that allows us to appreciate.

God does not make corn grow. God gives us the ability to be thankful when we work hard, and, due to various circumstances, we can grow corn. Corn would not grow without nature, but God gives us the mind to help us know how to plant the corn. Without God, we would probably think we did it all by ourselves, and there would be no thanksgiving. God is in the thanksgiving, the appreciation. Think of the ability to hear. Music can be played, but the real artist is the one who can hear and appreciate it. Without artistic appreciation, music may be all around us, and we may hear the sound, but not appreciate it.

God is that aesthetic appreciation that allows us to fall in love with life, which is the truth that makes us free. Imagine how many times you can show someone something good, and it's never seen if the person cannot appreciate it. On the other hand, imagine someone who can appreciate something good who has never seen it, yet can almost bring it into existence. That is what Jesus did. Jesus was saying, in effect, "I hear music that you don't hear. I am aware of things you do not see. I know what you have been taught, I know what you have heard, but I say. . . ." Jesus was presenting ideas and possibilities that he saw, but of which people were unaware.

When we see that Jesus struggled, trying to draw humanity to a larger awareness in life, we have every right to assume that God is like that as well. This kind of God is a redeeming God, rather than a God who is all-powerful, controlling, and punishing.

Sometimes we think that being God would be the most marvelous thing in the universe. Perhaps the only thing that keeps God sane is the fact that God loves. Look at our world. God is love, and that, to a large degree, is why God suffers.

We see God's suffering in the father of the prodigal son in the story Jesus told. There was a certain man who had two sons. One day the younger son came to his father and said, "Give me what is mine." Then the son took what he had and went into a far country. You can tell how far away he went because he ended up feeding swine, which meant that he, a Jew, was in Gentile territory. He went as far from home as he could go, not only geographically, that was minor, but also psychologically and spiritually.

The younger son was a long way off, and he wasted what he had. After some time, he was so hungry that he thought perhaps he could fill his stomach with the husks the swine ate. No one gave him anything. He began to think, "The servants in my father's house are better off than I am here. But there is no point in my thinking that I am a son any longer. I've acted like a fool. Let's face it; I've destroyed my relationship with my father."

So often we do not realize what we really want until we have lost it. That is the way we are, and that is the way this young man was. Therefore, he said to himself, "I'll go back to my father, but I won't ask him to take me back as a son. I've already acted foolishly enough." He was pompous and arrogant when he left home, but now he is very honest and open. He thought, "I'll go back and ask him if he will let me come back as a servant." That is swallowing your pride, is it not? He knew his elder brother was at home, and he probably knew what his elder brother's reaction to his returning would be.

Nonetheless, the younger son began his journey home. And, when he was a great way off, his father saw him and ran and fell on his neck and kissed him. Jesus used symbols at this point in the story, saying, "He put a ring on his finger," which was a sign of authority. "He put a robe on him," signifying that he was an honored guest. "He put shoes on his feet," meaning the son is not a slave. "He killed the fatted calf," which tells us he was going to have a banquet. Jesus chose symbols that were obvious to his listeners.

The prodigal son was going to beg for his father's forgiveness, but he never had a chance to make the speech he had prepared, because his father said, "This, my son, was lost and is found, was dead and is alive again." And that is a picture of God.

Another character in this story is the good, obedient elder brother. When we are good, we are also often judgmental. We are all like this at times, as we are all like the younger brother at other times—we want to take what we can and get away. We see characteristics of ourselves in both of the brothers.

When we are very judgmental, we look at our goodness and know we are capable of accomplishing many things. We think, "I'm not bad like someone else, particularly in that area. I have sins, of course, but they are not those sins."

The elder brother would not go into the house. A party was going on, and he stayed outside. He did not even refer to his younger brother as a brother. He said to his father, "This, your son, has come home, and you've killed the fatted calf. You've never given me a kid. Look at the difference. You've entertained him, and look at what you've done for me."

Out in the yard, the father visited with the elder son, saying, "All I have is yours. You've been faithful and dependable; that's right. Maybe you've sacrificed a lot to stay home, but everything I have is yours. Don't you understand that? Can't you get over your pride and your arrogance and the fact that in some ways you are better than your brother? Can't you realize that, in his badness, he might be better than you because he is now open and, therefore, can find what he wants? But your very goodness keeps you from being close to me."

Is it not strange that goodness can block us? That is almost shocking. The church asks you to be good. Throughout your life you have heard: "Keep the commandments; be good." But problems arise when you think you are the sole creator of goodness. This was true in the elder brother's case. His goodness kept him out in the yard; he couldn't go into the house and join in the celebration. He was outside, talking about his goodness, saying, "Look what I have done all my life. I have served you, God. Don't I deserve better than this?"

This is not true of the younger son in this story. He may have been spoiled for most of his life. He went away, wasted everything he had, and he suffered. But he grew up instead of dying in self-pity and cynicism. He said, "Why, I'll go back to my father, and I'll ask him to make me a servant."

We are going to suffer; there is no way to get around it. At times, if I could have my wish for you, I suppose I would pray that you would not get hurt. We can bring pain upon ourselves, sometimes other people bring it to us, and sometimes it is unavoidable. But we are going to be hurt. Perhaps the best prayer I could pray for you would be, "O God, when they get hurt, may they not be destroyed." This young man was hurt, and he remembered home. He was hurt, and he wanted to come home. He was hurt, and he started home. That is powerful.

God does suffer. We want to be in heaven with God when we die, but we never picture God as suffering. Yet, can you imagine God not suffering if God cares? If God is personal? If God knows? If God is aware? We need to allow God to be in the nature of Jesus as Jesus wept over the city of Jerusalem. The father in the story is hurt. His pain does not cause him to blame someone else and say, "Shame on you; you ought to be better. Look how I'm hurt." The father's hurt is redemptive. God suffers.

And we suffer; it is part of our existence. And God suffers, too.

Perhaps you are sick. Maybe you cannot get well, and you are aware of this. Maybe you are frightened; who wouldn't be? Perhaps someone you love is dying or suffering and a miraculous event is not taking place—there's a better miracle than that. You live in a miracle because you are with God. Again, God does for you what you cannot do for yourself—God gives you the strength to face what you knew you could not face. You thought, "Why, there is no way I can do that. I can't even say the right thing. I can't even talk without crying. I can't face it." And you do. Many of you have gone through this, or you have seen other people go through it.

You see, we meet the sacred in our own need. That is where we always meet God. I would have thought we met God in our goodness. I would have thought we met God where we are strong. We do. God is there, but we do not know it. We are deaf and blind to his presence. But when you are embarrassed or a failure, or when your success is so utterly empty, God meets you and you meet God, precisely where you fail and where you recognize that you are in need. That picture of God was given to us by the man Jesus of Nazareth.

2

What Is God Like?

To a great extent, regardless of our faith, many of us share the same concepts of God. Jesus knew how the people in his day perceived God, so he met them where they were in their thinking and tried to develop their understanding of the nature of God. That is often the way a good teacher works. He or she will begin with what a pupil knows and then take the student on an adventure. Following that, if the student is fortunate enough to grow, the student will see more than he or she has ever experienced.

In simplified form, let me describe three approaches that we make to religion. These ideas are not confined to the Judeo-Christian faith; they are true of other faiths as well. I think that one of these approaches or a combination of them is the way most people see their God.

Sometimes we perceive God as being over against us. That is true of so many Christians in America, I would imagine. We see God as the powerful one, while we are weak. God is strong, and we are bad; therefore, he is going to get us in trouble.

At other times, we view God as being capricious, unpredictable. We still see him as strong and powerful, but we cannot rely on him because we do not know what he might do next. Hence, we are afraid of God. And fear causes us to do all kinds of things—we will pray out of fear; we will give money out of fear. We want people to know that we are Christians, because we are frightened to death. We have committed some sin; we have done some things that are wrong; and we are threatened. The big strong God is over against us; he is capricious, and we are afraid.

There are times when our idea of God is almost folksy—he's the man upstairs, the chum. We think, "You and me together, Lord, you and me." This is an equalizing idea that diminishes God. We make him someone we can take by the hand and lead around. So, when we want something, we pray for it, and we get it. God is our valet. There is no respect, but we can use him. After all, we think we should use him because we are converted.

As we view God, there are two elements that continually affect us: reward and punishment. We are aware of reward and punishment in almost every area of our lives—in our families, in school, at work, and certainly in the mundane things we do. What is more routine than driving a car? Yet, if we are careless or if someone else is negligent, we can be hurt. Thus we are, in a sense, punished by our own carelessness or by someone else's.

All of us are cognizant of reward. When we do well, we expect to succeed, and we feel our success will be followed by recognition and compensation in proportion to the way we have performed. Reward and punishment are not bad. As a matter of fact, they are part of the fabric of society. These two elements are so much a part of our corporate consciousness that we really do not know how to think apart from them.

However, this mode of thinking is dangerous when we move into the realm of theology, into thinking about God and the nature of God. Reward and punishment affect our theological understanding tremendously when they should not enter into it at all. They need to be erased, eradicated. This would be a radical approach to the way we see God. Yet, it is absolutely necessary, it seems to me, if we are to develop a healthier idea of God and a healthier idea of ourselves.

The Christian term *grace* is the closest we come to trying to do away with the idea of reward and punishment. We say that God's grace is freely given to all of us. And then we execute a tricky backward mental maneuver, because by the time we finish interpreting grace, we earn it. Our explanation is that God's grace comes to us through faith in Jesus Christ, which means we have to have the faith in Jesus. And, our reasoning continues, if we have the proper faith, which is another form of earning it, we will be rewarded by God's grace. That rationale is not at all in keeping with the nature of God. The finest example that I know of to negate that representation of grace is Jesus' teaching in reference to the prodigal son.

Grace is not something you earn. It is not something you deserve or that you can demand and receive. Grace simply is. When the prodigal son started home and was met by his father, he was recognized as a son, not as a servant. The son expected to return home as a servant, if he would be accepted at all. But the father had seen the young man as his son all along. However, when the young man realized that his father saw him as a son, it changed the young man's idea of himself. The son did not go back home because he had faith in something, causing his father to have to take him back because of his faith. He went back stripped bare, vulnerable, with no defense for what he had done. His father's attitude toward him was what changed him, not his attitude toward his father.

Nonetheless, in Christianity we preach that if our attitude toward God is proper, through Jesus Christ, then God can take us back. That is the antithesis of the way God is. Oddly enough, perhaps unintentionally, we treat grace in the same way. We say that if we have the right faith in Jesus, then God accepts us back with his grace because we have qualified by our faith in Jesus. If that were the case, the prodigal son would never have gotten home. His return was not brought about by the way he saw his father, but by the way his father saw him. And the way his father saw him changed his idea of himself, which is what Jesus tried to do with people repeatedly.

As a matter of fact, I think perhaps Jesus' main purpose in life was to teach us the nature of God and to show us our true nature. Jesus tried to teach us that our enemy is never God. At times, our enemy may be circumstances or it may be our own creation or it may be someone else's doing. But God is always on our side, and never as noticeably so as when we are in such desperate need that we cannot do anything for ourselves.

We are aware of the idea that the physician comes for the sick and not for the well. Yet, we have developed a theology that almost translates this idea to mean that when you no longer need God and are very good, then God is certainly available to you. When you really qualify with a proper religious faith; when you qualify by receiving the holy sacrament; by the proper belief in the Bible; by the right under-standing of theology; by being orthodox, disciplined, Christian, and moral, then God is certainly available to you. You can then thank God. You are saved in this world and in the world to come.

Consequently, we have a reward and punishment system in relation to God, which reinforces our idea of reward and punishment in reference to people. We think that if God, being very gracious, can punish us because of our badness, then we can punish people because of their badness. This response indicates our lack of confidence in the fact that the badness is punishment itself. Think about this in regard to a liar. When someone lies, he or she becomes a liar. All the grace in the world does not negate that. The person is a liar. The grace of God may change the person, but the punishment is that you have become what you are.

Therefore, it seems to me that we do not have to levy more punishment. I am not speaking in legal terms, but in regard to our perception of God. We are afraid that people will not function well if we do not have the threat of punishment and the joy of reward. That is true with many people, which reveals that we have not evolved enough. Our ethical understanding of life, our appreciation of the quality of life, is way beyond our ability to perform.

Yet, that is the way progress comes about. We can dream of something before we find it. We can think ourselves into a better way of acting, and then we catch up with it. Someone dreams of a cure for a disease long before it is found. And so it is in living. I think it should concern us that we do not have that creative thought in terms of God or in terms of religion. We regress to the traditional stratagem of reward and punishment; we concoct a God to oversee that system; and then we are perfectly justified in building a society around that system.

We speak of God as being slow to anger. Implicit in this reference is the idea that God does become angry if we are bad enough long enough. Now, I assume most people would agree that the nature of God is merciful and that God has grace. But if you can alter the nature of God, if you can make God become angry by your badness, then you are stronger than God. You have changed the nature of God; you have changed what God normally would choose to be by your badness. Therefore, you have manipulated God. You have made God become angry, which must be an embarrassment to God. Now, carry this rationale a step further. If that is the case—if your badness makes God become angry—God, almost against his true nature, will begin to punish you because you are so bad.

Is that not a strange idea? Now you are bigger than God. Your badness controls God. Your badness is stronger than God's grace. I do not believe we are prepared to accept that conclusion, but that is what we are teaching when we state that God is slow to anger.

The truth is you can never wear down the grace of God. His grace remains in spite of the most heinous sins we can commit. The prodigal son is symbolic of every soul on earth. And the one thing that the prodigal son could not do was make his father deviate from giving his grace, love, and presence to his son.

Jesus was quite clear, and the nature of God is very identifiable. It is always redemptive, always compassionate, always concerned. His grace can wear out anything to the contrary just as truth can wear out a lie, just as beauty can wear out ugliness and love can wear out hate. God wins, not by resorting to a punishment or giving a reward; instead of a reward, it is the awareness of the nature of who you are.

When the prodigal son came home and his father recognized him as a son, that was not a reward. His sonship had always been his; it was not something his father gave him upon his return. His father had never changed. But when the young man came home and realized, "I am a son," his eyes were opened, and he became aware of what he had always been and of what his father had always been.

However, we are slow learners. Over a period of centuries, we have developed the idea of a God of reward and punishment. We think God may take us back if we sacrifice the right way. And we reinforce this notion by reading about Abraham offering Isaac to God, so that God might take Abraham back. The church gives credence to the idea of reward and punishment by saying, "Give your tithes to the church, and God will reward you. Pray properly, and God will grant your petition."

Instead, the church should be urging people to get in harmony. Prayer is important, but it does not change God. Prayer brings the person into harmony. This is similar to following sound principles of health. There is no magic involved. It is a law of harmony that when a person eats, sleeps, and exercises properly, that person is apt to be healthier than he or she would have been without doing these things. That is true mentally, psychologically, and spiritually. The reward, then, is not a gift that is given to you because you did well. The reward is a very natural part of your doing well.

In the same way, failure is a natural part of neglecting things. It is not a punishment; it is the nature of leaving things alone. If you do not tend your rose garden, it will be destroyed by aphids and weeds. It is not that you are punished because you did not care for the garden; the result is the very nature of what happens when you do not look after it.

We need to move away from the idea of reward and punishment in reference to God and think of God as the consistent presence, constant in grace, compassion, and love. Punishment does not come from God; punishment is the consequence of what we do. God is not punishing us because of the wrong things we do. God is trying to bring us out of the destructive nature we are following. The happiness, the joy, the healing, the health, and the strength that we have when we are in harmony are not rewards that God gives us. They are the natural consequences of following what is right. Jesus teaches this. God never changes. God is always with us to redeem us. No one can be bad enough to exhaust God's grace, so that God becomes angry and punishes.

Yet, these erroneous ideas, in varying degrees, creep into our thinking. So when we use the word *God* we have mental pictures of God. The way people saw God two thousand years ago is not unlike the way we see God today. And then Jesus came and taught. He did more than that, of course, but he did at least that. From my point of view, he could do no greater thing than teach about God.

Jesus was aware of God the Creator. He was Jewish, although we have almost stolen him from the Jews. The Christian takes Jesus and runs off with him, saying, "Here is my Lord. This is the only way you can get to heaven. You had better come to us if you are going to get to God." Jesus was a Jew. He was dedicated in the Temple when he was a small child. He grew up with Judaic ideas, with the Jewish thought of the world and of religion.

Since Jesus was Jewish, when he referred to God, he used, "He," the masculine pronoun: "He who sent me will send you another who will remain with you forever." Jesus referred to God in this sense. And then, over a period of time, he injected the idea of God the Father. When Jesus was around twelve years old, he was lost in the Temple. When Joseph and Mary found him, you know what he said: "Must I not be about my father's business?" He spoke of God as a father. There were, of course, people before Jesus who thought of God as being a father, but Jesus clarified this idea.

And then one day, at what seems to me to be the very peak of Jesus' teaching, apparently he had reached the place where he could express an idea the way he wished. In effect, the artist had found himself. He was not impressed by himself, but comfortable with himself. An idea had come of age, he could articulate it, and he was looking for people who could hear it. At this point Jesus told the story of the prodigal son, which, as we have seen, is really a story about God.

Doubtless, Jesus' disciples had been introduced to the idea that God was a father, and then one day Jesus turned to them and said, "I have called you my friends." Think of that! To me, that is the breakthrough. If I were to say what I think is the turning point in all theology, the greatest idea that I have ever run across in development, not by itself, but in the context of development, this is it.

You see, a father likes his child because he has to, or we think that is the case. You are his. Remember the story of the prodigal son: The young man has come back home, and there is the good father and the bad son, the big father and the unworthy person. That is the way it is. The father is on the throne; he is the man of the house, he owns the possessions. You wanted to be a servant, but he will show you how big and good he is—he will bring you back as a son. Nonetheless, there is still the big father and the little son. And then, aware of these complexities, Jesus said, "Now, I want to teach you something. That creative presence that you are aware of, that father concept of God, I want you to hear this: I have called you my friends. I have selected you; I am your friend, and you are my friend."

If you take that in a syllogistic way and work it backward, it means, "He who has seen me has seen the father; God is like I am." As Christians, we misread this. Jesus was too good to call himself God. Who do you think he was praying to when he was on the cross? God. But here, Jesus is saying, "I've come for a purpose. God is like I am in this sense. You are my friends, and God is like that." It is a friendly God. Think of that!

That is nonpareil teaching. Not only is it teaching at its best, but also that is the finest idea imaginable pertaining to people and their relationship to God. The idea was explained in a very simple way, the way great truths often are explained. False ideas can be explained in a very complicated manner, and someone can say, "Isn't he brilliant!" But harmony flows as you near the truth. What is more beautiful than something very simple? One flower, one child, one thank you, one smile, one look, one touch of the hand. This was very simple: "I have called you my friends."

With this statement and in other ways, Jesus clearly said that the creative process that brought the universe into existence is a friendly presence. Yet, the world does not believe that. The forces that control this world are not demonic. The only demon in the world is the one you conjure up in your own mind. The world is brought into existence by a friendly, caring, fatherly God. How do we know? Because Jesus taught it.

Now, if you do not want to follow what Jesus taught, fine. You have every right not to do so. But, in the name of Christianity, the moment you call yourself a Christian, you have to take the man's teaching seriously. He did not teach everything on the same level as if everything is of the same importance, but this is vital: The presence that brought all of creation into the world is a friendly presence. You can know that; you can verify it. Look at the harmony of life, the very balance. You have what you need. Someone can take it from you, of course, but the balance of nature almost leaves you in awe. You can depend upon it. It is not predictable; there are times when we have storms, and there are times when we are hurt. Nature doesn't always seem to be amicable, but we have minds that know how to cope. Therefore, nature is dependable, but not predictable. And the presence in that is a friendly presence.

Furthermore, you have been selected by that presence, God, because he has chosen you to be a friend. Jesus did this when he said, "I have selected you to be my friend." That is one of the highest compliments. Regrettably, there are times when the word *friendship* may not seem very enjoyable or desirable to some people. But what greater thing in the world could happen than to be asked to be someone's friend?

At a synagogue in Poland, years ago, a janitor who had worked there for a long time came to the senior rabbi one day and said he was going to change jobs. When the rabbi asked him why, the janitor said he had found another job and wanted to take it. One of the men of the synagogue had decided that he wanted to employ the janitor to work for him full time. He wanted the janitor to sit out on the highest hill to wait and watch for the Messiah, so that whenever the Messiah came, the janitor could come and tell the man, and the man would know it immediately. The rabbi said, "You don't want to do that. Stay here and work with us. You have a good job here." But the janitor argued that his present job might not be permanent. The rabbi promised him his present job for the rest of his life. Then the janitor protested that the building might burn down and they might decide not to rebuild, or the next rabbi might not want him to stay. The janitor concluded by saying, "I want something that is permanent, and, as long as I am sitting out there on the mountain waiting and watching for the Messiah, I will always have a job."

He was right, because it will never come. The Messiah will never come over a hill or appear on a cloud. I know there are passages of Scripture saying that, but they do not fit some other passages. Think it through. How does God work? How has he worked in your life? It's a cop-out to wait for the Messiah and let the Messiah do it. That is not what Jesus taught at all. He said, in effect, "You are good Jews, you are human beings . . . all of you are people. I want to tell you something. The whole universe that you see has been brought into existence by a friend, not by an evil mind, not by demonic forces. Can't you see the harmony of it? You are a part of that. That is a friend. But that, by itself, doesn't tell you enough. It is also a father. Maybe you have had some unhappy experiences with a father. You think your father has to accept you because he is your father. I want to go a step beyond that."

This is the breakthrough, the most refreshing thing that I know of in theology. I cannot imagine anyone focusing it more accurately than Jesus did, and he did it with clarity: "The creative presence that brought the universe into existence, which you sometimes call father, is your friend. Now, I have selected you. I have called you. You are my friends, and I am your friend. But don't stop with that. I want you to go out now and be a friend." That, I think, is really what Jesus taught about God.

3

The God You Already Know

⸙

*I*n regard to our awareness of God, I think we know far beyond what we are willing to admit. This is similar to the way a child begins to understand his parents. He is beginning to understand them; yet, he still clings to the ideas he thinks he ought to have in reference to them. Perhaps he realizes that his father cannot do everything, that his parents are not always right and they do make mistakes. As he becomes aware of this, he tends to resent them and almost wishes they could solve all of his problems. Later, if the child continues to grow, he realizes his parents labor with the same challenges and decisions as he does, only more so. Following this realization he may begin to have an appreciation for his parents that is larger than he ever imagined.

He now knows that his parents are in the struggle with him doing a far better job at times than he had any idea. His parents, he has become aware, were never parsimonious. He realizes that many times they wanted to do much more, not simply in terms of money, but in terms of decisions, strength, and guidance. It was not that they had great resources and were giving meagerly. They were using all they had. And then he begins to see his parents in a new light, out of the fact that they care for him, rather than the fact that they were powerful and could have made things better if they had wanted to.

In this sense, we understand God already. We know that God cannot bring about everything God wants in this universe. We surely understand that. If God could and God does not, then God is bad. We have a God who is not the omnipotent God, in the sense of being all-powerful, able to do everything. We have a God far more "powerful" than that, in terms of integrity and rightness.

Thinking of what we really know, we see that so often it is not so much a matter of being exposed to a new idea as it is allowing what is already there to surface. That does not mean we do not grow. Of course, we assimilate many more facts. But, by and large, our prejudices slip aside when we mature, and we obtain more truth as we move in a healthy direction.

Paul spoke of this when he said, in effect, "It is the God within you that I want to discuss. You may not even be aware of the sacredness within you. It is not God out there that you must be introduced to; it is that awareness of God within you, the creative presence of God within you. This is the God that has always been. You have temples to all of these gods. I want to talk to you and think with you about the unknown God that you are unaware that you already know."

So often, that is where truth is found. Perhaps someone who is irate, furious, could not let you know that he or she loves anybody; yet, you know this if you are perceptive. What do you do? You have to cut through a lot of things. You do not create the sacredness and put it in the person. Conversion does not do that; conversion allows the person to discover what has been there all along.

It seems to me that we can never tell a person anything unless that person is reasonably aware of the subject we want to discuss. For instance, you cannot teach physics to someone who cannot count or multiply. This is a stairstep; one leads to the next. The fact that we developed the wheel before we developed the motor is understandable. It was not that we had to have the wheel before the motor, it was the process of one vista allowing us to become aware of something else. So, intuitively, in the very innate situation in which we find ourselves, we know a lot of things we cannot assimilate.

Think of the words we use for things that we cannot bring into existence. We are aware of the word *happy,* but we do not have the capacity to bring happiness to everyone, and sometimes we do not know where to find it ourselves. We are aware of the word *peace* and what it means, but we may find and be able to experience very little peace in our lives. We cannot bring joy into existence, or love; yet, we use these words.

And in regard to God, we are already so far ahead

in our awareness that our awareness has outrun our experience. Therefore, we keep experiencing a God who is meager, small, and limited, because that is the God we reinforce to ourselves and teach to other people. But, in reality, we know better. Our minds and our intuitive nature have already outgrown that primitive understanding of God. God is bigger and better than we believe or think; we know that. Yet, we do not want to allow ourselves to give up the familiar, even though it is very small and parochial.

We must be aware that our God is bigger than our religious convictions and is concerned for the entire world. We need a world vision, and the day is coming when we will need a universal vision. God is all-encompassing; all humanity is dear to God, precisely because they are human beings. Religion needs to reinforce this. When that happens, dedication will come to the larger concept of God, rather than to the smaller. Regrettably, dedication is frequently to the lowest possible common denominator.

Obviously, Jesus was aware of God in a way that other people were not. In order to share his idea of God, he related to elements in the people's lives, such as in the analogy of the lost coin. He spoke of a woman losing a coin and going to look for it because the coin was important to her. People understood that. The woman apparently had a very limited income, so she looked until she found the coin. And Jesus was saying, in effect, "People are this way with God." If you have a great deal of money and lose one coin, it is not a significant loss. But when you do not have much, it becomes very important. Now, Jesus is saying, "Can you not understand, as the woman who didn't have much looked for the coin, that God is like this? Not because God doesn't have much or has everything. It's the very nature of God to want you to be with God. In the same way the woman needed the coin, you are important to God."

Jesus stressed the idea of how important people are to God. The people probably already knew that, but they could not accept it because of their culture, their fear, and their religious convictions. Jesus was giving people permission to catch up to their intuitive nature, to catch up with what they already knew.

The intuitive nature of people is probably a saving grace. We have already outrun our prejudice, or we can. We have already outrun our smallness, our parochialism. The intuitive nature within us has already outgrown the petty culture that we try to support. And once the mind, the psyche, and the soul have caught a glimpse of how things ought to be, we are restless until we work toward that. This is the way the kingdom of God can come upon the earth. We have been given a glimpse of it. Intuitively we knew it.

We always knew God ought to be a compassionate, caring God, the way Jesus showed, taught, and lived. We knew it then, and we know it now. But we resist this idea because power not only fascinates us, but it also is necessary to us. We hate to share power. We are threatened when we lose it. A change is a form of demonic experience to us. We want control, tranquility, and stability.

Still, intuitively we know that in order for the world to be alive, the renaissance, the new birth, has to break open the smallness that we tend to cling to and reinvent. We know that God is better than we teach, practice, or profess. The day will come when we can advance our culture to the place where we can begin to practice what we already know, which is real progress.

We have seen this advance in regard to slavery. The South knew slavery was wrong. By and large, they knew it, regardless of what they said and the steps they took to retain it. They said it was necessary. At times, they said it was of God; it was right. Basically they said it was economically necessary, but they knew the demise of slavery was around the corner. That is one reason why they were so afraid of anything that threatened this institution. They knew the day would come when blacks would not be enslaved. Therefore, they had to develop a society to allow that to be possible. The mind had already gotten there and, regrettably, for this country, it took a Civil War and so many other battles to try to bring about the possibility of appreciation among races.

Once you see the possibility of what should be, there is a restlessness that all the forces in the world cannot prevent from coming about. This is similar to something being announced. Then the idea is there, you have been introduced to it. Yet, you and I are not able to hear what we are not prepared to hear.

Consider how we think we begin to be aware of facts. Sometimes we believe things when we read them. Seeing something in print gives it credibility. Someone can say, "I read it in a book. It has to be factual." Perhaps it is true; perhaps it is not. As you mature, you begin to read with a more discerning eye. You are not becoming cynical, but you know something is not accurate simply because it is in print.

At other times, we believe things because we have heard them, particularly when we hear them from someone in whom we have a great deal of confidence. We may quote someone we believe in, saying, "I know it's true, because someone told me this, and I know that person would not have told me if it were not true." Frequently that is accurate, but not always.

Usually, I think, we fall into the trap of believing what we want to believe. We reveal a great deal about ourselves by doing this. We go by what we read and hear. We use our own minds, while, simultaneously, our psychological natures are working on us. So, we may be very objective at times, but at other times we are not. That is understandable; yet, in many instances, we report something the way we would like it to be. If a friend of yours is in trouble, you defend the person. If someone you don't care for is in trouble, you are almost glad the person has a problem. So often our response reveals where we are.

In dealing with a situation, there is a time when you and I reveal how we are. Think of what you wish you knew. This is particularly true when we are taking a test. It is true when we run in to someone we know and wish we could recall the person's name. There is information galore, and we feel, "If I could just have it at my fingertips. Or maybe I could recall it if I were given more time. If I were given the chance, I could look it up." Consider the things we would like to know.

There are also times in our lives when we know many things that we wish we did not know. That can be devastating. You may receive a report from a doctor; there is nothing good about it. You consulted the doctor hesitantly; you felt you should. Now you have found out something, and you wonder if you can handle it. I've known people in that situation. Usually they are giants, it seems to me, and handle a poor prognosis in an unbelievably remarkable way. Think of the information you sometimes get about a friend, someone whom you love very much and can say, in effect, "I wish I didn't know that." It is almost more than you can assimilate, very much like sound. If you turn sound up loud enough, at some point it becomes noise. A certain decibel is reached, and you cannot hear the sound any longer; you cannot assimilate it.

In addition, many times you know things that are irrelevant. They are of no consequence whatsoever. There are also things you will never know. Let us be honest—there are so many things that you and I live in faith, in belief. Can you prove that a brick is a brick or that it is raining? But faith enters when we move out into the depth and meaning of life. We really do not know a great deal. We know, and we do not know. What is the proof?

We take Jesus' word for something. Can we prove Jesus was right? He was killed. Can we prove it? We say he is resurrected and he lives. Can we prove it? Jesus said, "The world cannot see this." He did not mean you and me against the world, as in the song. That is not the way it is. What he was saying is very personal. There is a part of us that does not know.

41

There is a part of us that believes and longs to grow, and there is a part of us that is very small and prejudiced. It is not us against the world; it is us against ourselves. We want to be healthy, but not really. We want to be honest, but not all that much. We want to be caring persons; yet, at the same time, look at the avarice within our lives. It is not the world against us; it is that dark side against us.

Paul said, in essence, "It is the good within you that I want to cultivate. You do not even know it is there. Sometimes, in an egotistical way, you will think you have a great deal of it. At other times, when you disappoint and hurt yourself, you will think that God is not within you at all. I want to talk with you about the God you already know. Where do you find that God? Not in a monument, not in a building, not in a shrine, not in nature, not out there. It is that God within you which no one else can discover. That is what I want to think with you about—the God you already know."

If you were truly aware of the God that you already know, you would also know that you are sacred and that you belong to God. I don't know what you could say to a person in counseling that would be more significant than that. When someone is acting in a rather difficult, obnoxious way, at times we are inclined to say, "He or she is egotistical." That may be true, but often it is because the person is insecure. This behavior may indicate anything but caring too much for himself or herself. A secure person is not likely to be self-centered, because bragging isn't necessary. A secure person can feel perfectly comfortable. There is no need to overplay his or her hand. Hopefully, you know the security that is found when you feel you are going in the right direction.

This security is found in the honesty that comes to you when you are alone. At such times, you are not trying to deal with what other people may expect. You begin to realize that you belong to God; you actually do. That is not pride or arrogance; you simply belong to God. There is a sacredness within you, a quality of life within you; the capacity to love is within you. It has been there all the time. It comes from the God who has been there all the time. It is that presence of God that Paul said he wanted to discuss. It is the God within you that you cannot know in the sense of seeing, but you know in the sense of being aware.

Not only do you belong to God, but everyone belongs to God as well; every living person is sacred. I believe a great contribution can be made to life in terms of competition. In an economic system, the way we operate at least, competition seems to be basic to our society. There is nothing wrong with competition if it is meant in terms of trying to do a better job, in terms of quality and offering a better product at a better price.

But competition can be used destructively. The very nature of our economic system can be to destroy the competitor; the competitor becomes the enemy. I am not suggesting that we become flaccid, that we give everything we have to someone else who is in the same position in another company. Not that at all. But in the long-run, other people have to prosper if you are going to prosper.

We cannot live as an individual unit. If our country is going to be strong, other countries need to be strong. If you are going to have a healthy neighborhood, your neighbors need to be healthy. You are a part of the human race. We live in a world—one world, really, one humanity. There is nothing new about that. We have known it all along, but we tend to forget it. Perhaps we recognize this fact only in fear or out of necessity.

When a tornado wreacked destruction, which was not the will of God but a natural disaster, God was hurt because God loved the people. Think of the times throughout history when people were living and struggling as we do in our own lives when a bomb dropped. The people huddled; they ran. They wept, and they died. We caused it, or some other country caused it. But we justify this by thinking, "That is an enemy, and, after all, we must take care of the enemy." You and I can live like that, and we'll produce another generation who will live like that. If they don't destroy themselves, they will produce another generation who will live the same way. It will go on that way because it has gone on like that for so long.

And over against that, thank God, Paul spoke, saying, "It is that unknown God I want to talk with you about. You do not find it in your shrines or in your buildings or in your cathedrals, temples, or churches. You do not find it out there. You find it in your own life. You are sacred. It is that unknown God within you, and that God is within every one of you."

Go ahead; run from God. Lie, or do whatever else.

We really want to be healthy, caring, giving persons. We want to care; we want to love. We want to be better than we are. To this end, remember what Paul said, "I want to talk with you about the God that you already know."

4

The Difference Between God and the Devil

American Christianity sees very little difference between God and the devil. Yet, despite what is often taught, I do not believe there is a personal devil. There is only one god, which is God, that creative presence. We might as well acknowledge forty gods if we accept two. Whatever works against God is demonic, but that opposition is not represented by a personal god called the devil or Satan. The idea of a continuing war between God and the devil is found in classical Christianity and in portions of the Bible, but that is a misconception, a misrepresentation. A war between God and the devil is an accurate biblical statement, but the writers of the Bible were mistaken when they wrote this description of God. If justification is needed to take on Scripture, Jesus did it repeatedly.

He took on the Torah, and he would take on the New Testament if he were here today. Jesus understood that truth is never a position; it is always a direction.

However, for the purpose of discussion, I will use the word *devil* in a symbolic way. Now, what is the difference between the way you see God and the way you see the devil? In all probability, there is very little difference. You may say that the devil offers you all kinds of rewards and marvelous experiences. He is a hearty advocate of the "enjoy now, pay later" plan. Yet, you are also taught that the devil deceives you and leads you into trouble. You may also say the devil has power. Many of us refer to the devil's control by saying, "The devil made me do it!" In other words, we believe a large number of the problems in the world are caused by the devil. If this is true, we think there will be healing in the world if we can eradicate the devil.

One of the world's religious leaders recently said that the main issue we now face is the control of the devil. That is not true. If the gentleman meant this symbolically, he may have had a point. But there is not a devil who is causing events or wreaking havoc. Quite obviously, there are demonic things in the world, but we cause them; people are responsible. Yet, a devil is presented to us, and one attribute of that devil is power.

Along with a powerful devil, we are shown a God with power. God is described as being able to do anything he wants to do. It is said that God will eventually reward you if you follow him. If you choose not to follow him, he will consign you to hell. This is the diorama that is created for us of the battle between the two gods.

In order to see a more accurate picture of God, we do not need another translation of the Bible; we need a different interpretation of the Scripture. A different thought pattern is necessary. We need to let Jesus teach us what he taught in the first place. For example, when we read or hear the story of David and Goliath, we think it was God's will that David killed Goliath. We believe God gave little David the strength to kill a giant. A more appropriate understanding of this story would be that while David may have had more right on his side than Goliath did, murder was not the will of God; God also cared for Goliath. This has to be crystal clear. When we read the New Testament, we should be aware that God loved Judas, according to the teachings of Jesus, as much as God loved Jesus. That is the way love works.

Jesus said that the greatest among you is the servant, that the physician goes to where there is need. Current interpretations reverse this, implying that we find God when there is not a need. We find God when we get pure enough.

Today many people insist that the only way to read the Bible is to interpret it literally. A literal interpretation of the Bible so often misses the meaning; it rules out the possibility of hearing what is unsaid. Has someone who loves you ever said to you, "Leave me alone! Just go away and leave me alone"? If you hear that only literally, you may go away and actually leave the person alone. In reality, what the person so often means is "Do not leave me alone." Frequently we mean just the opposite of what we say. This is the way we can speak to each other, and we have almost a spontaneous understanding of this in human interchange. Therefore, we should understand that literature is so often like this because literature deals with people. We need to hear the Bible in this sense. It is not a simplistic book; it is complex. Therefore, we need to give it an opportunity to express itself. We need to hear it in a more amplified way, rather than diminishing its meaning by taking it literally.

Our touchstone in reading and interpreting the Bible is always the goodness of God. God has always been as Jesus taught. This is true regardless of whether we are aware of it or not. Therefore, when we read that David killed Goliath and the Hebrews rejoiced, we can see that is understandable from the Hebrews' point of view, but not from God's point of view. A literal reading tells us that since the Hebrews hated the Philistines, God hated the Philistines. That kind of syllogistic reasoning is erroneous. The Hebrews' disdain for the Philistines was a result of their prejudice. Our bias today is often rooted in prejudice, too. But making God in our image in this regard is totally unacceptable. Yet, we have done this repeatedly under the guise of good biblical scholarship.

If the Bible did not imply a larger picture of God, it was due to the shortsightedness of the writers. Think of the story Jesus told about the good Samaritan, telling us that our neighbor is the one who needs us the most. Now go back and read about David and Goliath and the Philistines. Was Jesus correct in the New Testament? If Jesus was right, was God not the same way in the Old Testament? The difference is that Jesus knew it, and David did not. This fact does not make the New Testament better than the Old

Testament, because some very small, pious, narrow concepts are also found in the New Testament.

Nonetheless, we need to allow God to be good because God is bigger than our understanding of Scripture or Scripture itself and, quite obviously, bigger than we are.

But despite the fact that God is so much bigger than our interpretation of Scripture we continue to limit God. Many do this by espousing the idea of the ultimate battle of Armageddon. The name *Armageddon* is a derivation of Megiddo, a town in north central Israel. The Plain of Esdraelon, where numerous battles have been waged across the centuries, encompasses Megiddo. Solomon fought a battle there that can be read about in the Old Testament.

Later, the thesis was developed that the last battle of the world would be fought at Armageddon. And today we often hear, "We are getting set for the final battle, the battle of Armageddon, which will be between God and the devil. The battle will be horrible, and blood will flow up the horses' necks. But God will win; God will destroy and chain the devil. Then those whom God chooses, those who believe in God, will be called up to heaven where they will reign forever with God. The other people will be consigned to hell forever."

If we are reading the Bible with the goodness of God in mind, what is moral, redemptive, or spiritual about that idea? Napoleon and Hitler acted in a similar manner; they had banquets with those who helped them win battles. Jesus asked a probing question: "If you are nice to the people who are nice to you, what makes you different from the heathen? Do you think God is only nice to people who are nice to God? That God rewards the people who are his people and destroys those who are not?"

Here again, in the story of the battle of Armageddon, we have taken the word *God* and given it the qualities of a devil. And then we have told this story throughout America; we have told a tale about a god with satanic characteristics and called it Christianity. What is the difference between God and the devil? The way we interpret Scripture today, there is sometimes hardly any difference at all.

It is interesting to notice that Jesus did not fight back when he was arrested in the Garden of Gethsemane. I would not suggest that we always follow his example here. If your family is being attacked, of course, you should defend your family. Jesus was not married; he did not have a family in this sense. I do not believe he would have asked anyone else to do what he was doing. He knew what the outcome was going to be, and he was facing it personally. The soldiers arrested Jesus, and he did not use the conventional defense of his day. He used kindness, which was revolutionary. Was this successful? No. The soldiers crucified him.

Jesus did not win on that particular day. Or did he? Once a truth is announced, it is eternally true, and it will eventually expose everything else that is a lie. Kindness is right. It does not have to win.

What happens to anger, to war in the long-run? Does war not create more war? Does one battle not bring about another battle? Try waging a mini war on your family. You may win because you can fight or because you have the clout. And by doing this you may make enemies of everyone in your family. Now they are afraid of you; their fear lets you control them. But what does that mean?

What is more destructive than appetite and greed? Perhaps we can see greed for what it is by likening it to trying to compliment someone who is starved for compliments. You cannot say enough kind words. The person always has to ask for one more expression of approval.

At some time, both individually and collectively, both as a church and as a nation, we must separate God from the demonic so that it is the God of the Old Testament and the God of the New Testament who comes to save us. Jesus indicated what he thought was important when he asked Peter, "Do you love me?" "Yes," Peter replied. "Then," Jesus said, "feed my sheep."

In the light of that, what is God concerned about? Is making America wealthy the main concern of God? Is making believers in Jesus succeed, and all meeting at the top what our world needs? If we say that is what is in the mind of God, we are lying and making God the devil. Jesus was very clear when he talked about God and life. He said, "Now, inasmuch as you do it to people who cannot pay you back, you are doing it for God. They cannot reward you; they cannot promote you; they cannot give anything."

Now, what happens when you really care, when you want to do more but cannot? Perhaps you want to help someone who is lonely or somebody in your family who needs you. Maybe you want to help someone who is thoroughly obnoxious, someone who is brazen or rude. You may want to reach out because you have been where that person is and, in the name of God, you know you needed someone to reach out to you. You need someone to reach out to you when you are unlovable. You may want to help and not know how, but you start. If this is the case, what kind of a reward do you receive? You do not get bigger barns or more grain. You do not get a more expensive house or a finer automobile. It is far better than any of those. What you receive is found in the biblical message; it is found in the life of Jesus; and it is found in your life—you become a caring person.

5

The Danger of Using God

*W*hen you get ready to leave Egypt, take all you can from the Egyptians!" According to the Old Testament story, that is what God told the Hebrew people to do. Those instructions probably came as no surprise to the Hebrews, because such an injunction was in keeping with their understanding of God. God was not really saying this to them; yet, this is what they thought in much the same way that we can worship our personal desires and call them God.

In essence, this is what was written and attributed to God: "The king of Egypt will not give you leave unless he is compelled to do so. Therefore, I will stretch out my hand and assail the Egyptians with all the miracles that I will work among them. After that, the king will send you away. Further, I will bring this people into such favor with the Egyptians that when you go, you will not go empty-handed. Every woman shall ask her neighbor or any woman who lives in her house for jewelry of silver and of gold, and clothing." Notice these words, "Load your sons and daughters with them,and plunder the Egyptians."

Now, according to your understanding of God, do you think it is possible that he said that? You may say, "That's literally true; that is the way God is. The Hebrews belonged to God, and the Egyptians were bad, so God was saying to the Hebrews, 'I am going to arrange it so you can take advantage of them.' " If that is your reply, think of what some of the prophets later said about the nature of God. What does God want you to do, trick people? Does God want you to be religious so you can take advantage of others? Not on your life. What does the Lord require of you but to do justice, to love mercy, and to walk humbly with God?

Nonetheless, many times we worship our own desires and call them God. The Bible reveals the truth of God. Not every passage in the Bible shows the nature of God. In fact, quite often a passage shows what people thought God to be. Frequently, Jesus' teachings and actions were contrary to the Scripture. But, instead of following what Jesus taught, we make him conventional and use this interpretation to lie to ourselves.

One of the most apt illustrations of following our personal desires and saying we are following God is found in the New Testament when we read about the man whom we refer to as the rich farmer. He simultaneously talks to himself and prays, saying, "When I look at all I have, the land, the stock, the grain, I tell myself how very fortunate I am. God has blessed me." Is that not the way you and I so often think? We prove God by saying, "Look how lucky I am. See what God has given me." That is not the way Jesus proved God. Jesus would not prove God by an accumulation of things, but by compassion, by love, by mercy, by a quality of existence. As a matter of fact, Jesus saw a danger in just accumulating things. Things are fine, provided we use them for the purpose for which they are to be used. However, you know what we do—we worship the things. And the rich farmer said, "Now I will say to myself, 'I will build larger barns. And then I will say, 'Take thine ease!' "

Every last one of us is in danger of wanting to be in the rich farmer's position. We would be fools to want to suffer or be hurt. But do we really think we can diminish all of our fears and phobias by gathering enough things together? Do we not live in the world? What about our obligation to other people? What about love? What about relationships? Jesus' response to the rich farmer is a theological statement that is worded, in essence, "What a fool you are. Tonight your soul is required of you. Then what good will these things be?"

We interpret that response in a conventional sense as meaning, "You had better be converted to Jesus. The trouble with this man is he had all those things, but he was not converted to Jesus." Yet, we can be converted to Jesus and act just as the farmer did. As a matter of fact, the argument that so many use to convince people they ought to be converted to Jesus is "Get converted to Jesus, and you can build bigger barns and have more things." It seems to me that belief cuts against the very essence and truth of Christianity.

Nonetheless, we continue to use God. We do so by creating a God we want and worshiping him rather than trying to find God. This is especially true in America, where we concoct a religion that reinforces our selfishness. When I study our country's history, I have an idea that there is a greater emphasis on selfishness than there has ever been before. Granted, in the past, preachers utilized the idea of personal gain, saying you will be successful if you believe in Christ. But I have not known that idea to be preached as often and as fervently as it is today. Neither, to my knowledge, has it ever had so many adherents. We have a success-oriented religion that tells us we had better be suspicious of our religion and ourselves if we are not doing well. Consequently, we say you need to be converted to get ahead.

Religious highs are not the answer; quality is what matters. Do you care? Do you have compassion? The injunction found in the Old Testament, "Now go load your sons and daughters with this jewelry," does not reveal the nature of God. Those words tell us what the Hebrews thought God was like, but they were wrong in their thinking. God was not telling the Hebrews how to take advantage of the Egyptians. If the Egyptians were wrong in taking advantage of the Hebrews, would the Hebrews not be wrong in trying to take advantage of the Egyptians?

When we use God, when we concoct a God for our side who will be exactly what we want God to be, I think this encourages us to lie to ourselves. Let us say we decide we know God, and God is for our group only and we are for God. This relationship, to a great extent, excludes the social gospel. Therefore, the primary goals in our lives are for us to be successful and make more money, for our family to be well and healthy, and for us to do as we please. We can be giddy about all of this, if that is really what we think God is concerned about.

That is not the truth, but we will lie to ourselves. We will make it the truth, and then we can pretend we are generous when we are not. We will pretend we are involved when we are distanced. We will pretend we care. We will begin to lie to ourselves. We will think we care about our families, when we are not spending any time trying to adjust ourselves. We will know we are right because we have prayed about it. We read the Bible, and we are converted. In a sense, we are worshiping ourselves and calling it God. We deceive ourselves, and we develop a kind of religion that reinforces and justifies the deception.

When we deceive ourselves, we can play a religious game. We begin the game by making up our minds as to what we want, which is what happened to the Hebrews. Think of the many reasons they could find for justifying what they were doing: They had suffered for so long; they were slaves; they were captives in Egypt, and it seemed they would never be free. They had obvious problems, so they needed a God to help them. In order for God to help them, God had to belong to them, and they had to belong to God. God had to be on their side, and they had to be on God's side. That thought led to the Hebrews' concluding, "God doesn't care for the Egyptians; God is for us. God is going to help us, and God is going to get even with the Egyptians. Therefore, God has told us to take all we can from them."

They did not call it stealing, trickery, or manipulation. Instead, they said, "It is the will of God. God has told us to do this—every Hebrew woman is supposed to go to her neighbor, to any Egyptian woman, and ask to borrow silver and gold jewelry, then load it on her own children. The Hebrews are to plunder Egypt." Yet, in the classical interpretation of this story, we read that the Hebrews carried nothing when they left Egypt. They did not have time to get ready, so they took the unleavened bread. This version of their experience is remembered by the Passover. We can read two distinctly different stories of the same experience in the Bible.

So, when someone asks, "Do you believe the Bible?" and the reply is "Yes, I believe every word in the Bible," what does that really mean? Does it mean that every word shows you the nature of God? Of course not. This Old Testament story does not depict the nature of God. But it is an accurate picture of the nature of the way people act when they are hurt. When someone hurts you, intentionally or otherwise, you are embarrassed and you suffer. You sit back for a while and decide, "That person is my enemy; that person doesn't like me. I'm a good person. I'm religious. I know what I'll do—I'll get even with the person. That is what I must do. I must teach that person a lesson." At times, after thinking this way for a while, you can justify your retribution by concluding it is of God. You can even come to believe that God is telling you to get even with that person because that person is wrong.

This is not a new idea; stories of retaliation are found in the Bible hundreds of years before the birth of Jesus. What happens to us? In American religion today, if we are not careful, instead of worshiping an ethical God, a God bigger than our *ism,* a God bigger than Christianity or Judaism or the Muslim faith or anything else, instead of worshiping a God concerned about compassion and quality, we concoct a God who meets our own desires. Then we worship our desires and call them God.

Unfortunately, I do not think there is any way we can get around the idea of using God. We are going to do this, and we need to realize it. After realizing this, then periodically we need to push God away from us so we can see in terms of, "What am I doing? How does it look in the light of love or compassion?" Not, "Am I successful?" Not, "Am I aware of God?" Not, "Do I feel converted?" So often, those are not the right questions. The question is "How does this measure up in terms of compassion, fairness, love, or healing?"

Asking the right question is not as easy as it sounds because all of us are interested in ourselves. Quite obviously, we would have a multitude of problems if we were not interested in ourselves to some degree. We may realize that there is no one single good note on a piano. If the piano is in tune, one note is as good as any other note. The blend and arrangement of the notes produce the harmony. And so it is with an emotion and a feeling. A feeling by itself is not necessarily bad. Fear is not always bad. There are certain things that we ought to fear in order to survive.

However, we develop a certain pattern in life and assume that some things are good and that their opposites are bad. We can assume that self-preservation is always good, but it is not. On the other hand, to negate ourselves would certainly not be desirable either. But self-preservation alone, if it is not balanced by an awareness of what goes on in the lives of others, is very narrow and deceptive and ultimately becomes destructive. Our individual preservation depends to a great extent on the preservation of other people. Therefore, we should be on guard against this selfishness, this me-ism that permeates our existence. Self-centeredness allows us to use God on our behalf, which eventually becomes ruinous. We are in danger of using God in a destructive way if we do not stop trying to get by with everything we possibly can. We stop only if we are prevented by force. Our ethics, integrity, or choices do not deter us. Nonetheless, each of us wants self-preservation; we have vested interests. There is no way to get around that, and there is nothing wrong with it. You are yourself. You are dealing with yourself when you want to be converted, when you want to become better educated. There is no way to despise yourself and be healthy. You should love yourself, but also realize there is always a need to watch your appetite or you will destroy yourself.

What does that mean to us? We must protect ourselves. We understand that. Still, out of the desire to protect ourselves, out of the desire to be number one, over against that, we long to love, to care, to be involved in life, and to do a lot of things that are good. Therefore, rather than worshiping our desires and calling them God, we really long to worship God.

And in order to worship God and to be healthy, I think we need to try to find truth. We should fall in love with truth, with beauty, with goodness. Out of that, we find God. If we are converted to God and do not change the quality of our understanding of life, we will worship God in our own image and never know we have done it.

This is what happened to the Hebrews so long ago. Did they not worship God? Of course, they did. They longed to be with God. That was the only way they could find their freedom. Then what happened? "Since you are close to God, go rip off the Egyptians; trick them. Get the gold and the silver and load them on your own children. Plunder the Egyptians."

That is one way to look at it, but that is not God's way. That is the way we are, time and time again. Using God, it seems to me, is one of the dangers in our effort to be religious in America today. We worship our own desires and pass this off as the worship of God.

6

Beyond Proof

*P*roof can hamper progress, hinder achievement, and limit faith. Yet, all of us share a common desire for security and proof. We become confused in this day and time. What can we be assured of? What is reliable? These questions have been asked throughout history.

The exemplification of this desire for proof and assurance is seen in children, and, despite the passage of time, we never outgrow this longing; perhaps we should not. It is a part of our very nature as human beings. But, like so many other things, it can become destructive unless we counter and balance it with something else. We want proof in the realm of religion. We want the results of a litmus test to assure us that our side is right and is going to win.

And we develop our theological beliefs in order to support this desire.

The New Testament was written, to a great extent, to fit the Old Testament. Writers of the New Testament knew the Old Testament quite well. They looked for predictions and passages in the Old Testament, and then, time and again, made the New Testament fit what had been predicted.

At one point in the Old Testament, Isaiah is dealing with people, writing about their understanding of and response to God. Isaiah has the people demand, "Give us proof. Let us know that you are God. If you are God, let us know it. Show us something that we can rely on." And then Isaiah speaks for God, saying, "The Lord speaks and says, 'I will give you a sign. And this will be the sign you can rely on: A woman will conceive and bear a child.'"

What kind of a sign is that when birth is utterly routine, so ordinary? It is as if God is saying, "The sign is that there is no sign." That is the way I like to interpret this. What is the proof of friendship? You cannot prove it, although you can try to do so with symbols or demonstrations. What is the real proof of love? How can you possibly prove it?

Nonetheless, this "sign" is picked up on in the New Testament, where it says that Jesus is the child the prophet Isaiah was talking about. Now Mary becomes the woman and Jesus becomes the child, which takes some kind of a leap of faith. Isaiah said a woman would bear a child and there would be a leader. That was something he longed for and expected. Today, in much the same way, we could say the same thing. Surely women are going to continue to bear children, and I could say that two hundred years from now there will be a child born who will be a world leader. But my saying this does not make it happen; it will occur as events unfold.

The New Testament writers found it necessary to prove Jesus with identifiable, objective truth. People then and now are not necessarily impressed by his teachings. People are impressed by his performance of miracles, his supernatural powers, and that he was ordained of God, so he had to be the Messiah. Jesus is the Messiah, but not for any of those reasons. He is the Messiah because he happens to be the one who best shows us God. By best, I mean Jesus shows us God in terms of love, compassion, and ethics. He shows us a God of morality. That, within itself, is more profound and miraculous than foreordination, tying Jesus on to Mary with God being the father through the virgin birth.

Think of the Grand Canyon. It is obvious and all of our explanations of the Grand Canyon are rather secondary. The Grand Canyon sits in judgment on everything we say about it, as does Jesus' life. Jesus' life and teachings outrun all other kinds of proof; therefore, verification is unnecessary. Yet, we want to use Isaiah's statement to prove the birth of Jesus, and we want to use the physical resurrection to prove his significance. And then we can say that Jesus is of God for these identifiable, objective reasons, the way a convert might argue from the standpoint of apologetics. But far more significant than that, it seems to me, is the very nature of who Jesus was.

Ultimately, you go beyond your proof if you live by faith. The trouble with proof is that it limits faith. Suppose I say to you, "I want you to be my friend, and you must prove it daily." There is no way you can convince me you are my friend if I perceive you not to be. My method of testing you would limit my ability even to know who you are, because I am so determined that you fit my proof. Therefore, if you do not fit my proof, you cannot be my friend.

Proof can limit; it can damage. Proof, at times, destroys what it is trying to find. It blinds us to what we so desperately seek. If we set out to prove something, the process of proving can make us stop too early. We prove Jesus by the virgin birth. We prove that Jesus is the Savior by the physical resurrection, knowing perfectly well that we then have to get rid of the physical body and go on to other things. If we are going to live by faith, we outgrow the physical proof or the rational proof, in a sense.

From the Christian point of view, we talk about the Hebrews' missing Jesus, because they had a preconceived idea of the Messiah as being an earthly Messiah, and Jesus was not one. In a sense, they missed the one they were looking for because of a preconceived idea. The Christian can see the fallacy of demanding proof that fits the pattern in regard to Judaism. Yet, we turn right around and are so blinded to our own understanding and faith that we do not realize this same handicap applies to us. On one hand, we teach the idea that Jesus is going to usher in a messianic kingdom, saying the same thing that we criticize the Jew for. Some quarters of Christianity say the power of God will be exposed and God will establish his kingdom here on earth. Or we push Jesus out to a spiritual realm in a way that we cannot prove. There is no benchmark for Jesus' spiritual kingdom when, in reality, on a worldwide basis, we can see things are not that much better.

There has been no great change in events since Jesus' birth. As a matter of fact, there are strong arguments that we have been more hateful to one another in the last two thousand years than we ever were before.

What Jesus did was let loose ideas—an understanding of humanity that provided dignity for all people, an awareness of a compassionate God. How we handle these ideas will be our salvation or demise. The most significant things we can experience in life are beyond proof. You cannot prove friendship or love or a child's worth or the significance of an older person. Think of an elderly person who requires constant care. This involves time, effort, financial expenditure, and sometimes physical exhaustion. Nothing about this makes sense. The person cannot even thank you; there is no identifiable reward. There is certainly no joy in this responsibility, as far as empirical awareness is concerned. But someone happens to love that older person; there is a relationship that defies proof. Experience takes us way beyond proof, which is so necessary. Regrettably, religious faith demands proof, and faith ceases to be faith and limits religion when it demands proof.

The contradiction between demanding proof and religious faith should be stressed. Faith appreciates experiences, but it does not allow them to become proof. Faith allows experiences to become vistas, so we can continue to appreciate the experience, but we can also look to larger areas. A developing friendship with one person should enhance your ability to care for someone else without diminishing the friendship with that one person. And, in this process, perhaps you are introduced more completely to yourself.

It seems to me that whatever deadens awareness is

destructive and demonic. And what makes awareness more likely and helps us become more sensitive
to life is a form of being alive. If you are slowly
freezing to death, you reach the point where you do
not want anyone to awaken you. You want to be left
alone. At this stage, you are so comfortable in your
destruction that you almost treat death as redemp-
tion. To be brought back to life is so very painful that
you resent it. Oddly enough, as you come back to life,
the pain of being alive is almost overbearing. And
yet, it is life again.

We think of comfort as desirable, which it certainly
is, and we think of pain as something we want to
avoid. Awareness, at times, is like waking from a
serious illness. It is very painful. We become aware of
the world, of problems, and of things we cannot
handle. Therefore, we are inclined to face only what
we think we can solve, which means we want to see
very little, because we have very little equipment
with which to react.

But, like it or not, we happen to be in a world that is
extremely complex. We share this earth with billions
of people and, until we can become more aware of the
larger areas, we cannot handle the smaller areas.
There is a time when you feel you would be happy if
you could just mark off the human race and live by
yourself. But in running from everyone, you are
thrown back on yourself, and the haunting experience of being alone is so frightening that you find you
have to go back and face issues.

Eventually, we live on trust, on faith, and we live
on the possibility of growth, being aware of what
little proof we might have as a stepping stone. When
the greatest growth experiences of our lives take

place, we are probably unaware of them. We may have seen these experiences as mundane. Then, we look back upon them to realize that something larger has taken place.

Jesus is beyond proof in much the same way that all marvelous people are beyond proof. We do not prove Einstein. We can study Einstein and know something about his life, but we cannot prove him by simply looking at his genealogy and predicting the inevitability of his being Einstein. That is also true in the life of Abraham Lincoln. As a matter of fact, if Einstein and Lincoln had failed to be the Lincoln and the Einstein we know, by virtue of looking at their backgrounds, we would be justified in saying that we had no right to expect them to make any great contribution to life. All great people go beyond proof, as do the wonderful everyday experiences that we share with those who are important to us. The really grand things in life are those that do not rest on proof. They rest on being fortunate, being receptive, and being aware. Later, you can look back upon them and probably have the capacity to say, "Thank God that was a part of my life."

We live in a time of anxiety; that has always been true. On the one hand, there is definite proof that we want to clutch and cling to. On the other hand, there is hope. In the meantime, we live in anxiety. We may be waiting for a telephone call, a letter, or a doctor's report. Are things going to be all right? In addition to all of that, we want a religious experience that lets us know God is on our side and we are on the side of God.

According to the story, John the Baptist was standing in the River Jordan when Jesus and some other people approached, walking close to the shore.

John the Baptist is supposed to have said, "Behold the one who comes toward me; I am not worthy to loose his shoes. I am not worthy to be his servant." Then Jesus asked John to baptize him. During the baptism, the Scripture says very clearly, a dove descended from heaven, and the people heard a voice saying, "This is my son, in whom I am well pleased."

Would that not be a sign? Would that not be proof if it had happened that way? If that were the case, would you not think John the Baptist would be convinced forever? As an old man, he could have said, "I know. I baptized him and I heard a voice and I saw a dove coming from heaven. Jesus is the Messiah."

However, some time later John the Baptist was in prison. Perhaps, he was thinking he would not be allowed to live very long. Therefore, he really wanted to know whether God had acted; he wanted some proof. So John the Baptist sent one of his disciples to ask Jesus if he were the one, or whether they should look for another. Would John have done that if he had really heard a voice from heaven or seen a dove? That was a poetic way of speaking, but now John was asking for proof. So his disciple went to Jesus and asked, "Are you the one, or should we look for another?" And Jesus replied, in effect, "Go tell John this: This is a sign. Go tell him the good news is preached to the poor."

That is like saying a baby is going to be born. What is unusual about that? Nothing, really. Some people were getting well; some were not, but they all needed the love of God. "Go tell John the Baptist what you have seen, what you have experienced." Was there any sign? Not really; no proof. We join John the Baptist and long for proof, understandably so; yet, we have to live beyond proof as far as the greatest things in life are concerned.

I once taught a class dealing with the idea of the world that shaped the Bible. From our perspective, although we know better, we probably assume the Bible was given to us intact from God. Actually, the Bible was honed, hammered out of life over a long period of time. The stories in the Old Testament were told repeatedly, from generation to generation, in much the same way that we tell stories in our families. We repeat what family members have done, and we laugh about some events. We relate occurrences that are important.

At long last, the biblical stories began to be written. The first book of the Old Testament, the way we would refer to it, may have been written about 550 B.C. The last book was written a few hundred years later, before the Maccabean period, probably sometime around 200 B.C. The first book of the New Testament was not written until several years after Jesus was crucified. One of Paul's letters was probably written about fifteen years after the crucifixion of Jesus, around A.D. 45, and the last book of the New Testament was written around A.D. 110 or 115. Hence, the whole New Testament was written during perhaps seventy years; the Old Testament over several hundred years.

During those times, do you think society was always the same? Of course not. There were wars, battles, and political developments. The Bible was affected by the way people thought at the time it was written. And when you read it, it is being affected by how you happen to feel, by how you think, and by who you are. If we were to discuss the Japanese today, surely we know that in all probability our discussion would be in a different context than it would have been if it had taken place on December 8, 1941. The Japanese are the same people, but our discussion is taking place in a different situation.

We want proof from the Bible. What kind of proof did Jesus offer? People heard him from their own perspectives when he taught, preached, and talked. Jesus spoke, and different groups, different pockets of people heard him from wherever they happened to be. We are familiar with the Pharisees. They were an influential group of people whom we tend to think of as having been obnoxious. Yet, religiously speaking, they were probably the best people of that day. They not only believed in keeping the written law, but they also believed in keeping the oral interpretation of the law. As a result, they had thousands of laws to keep. There was no way anyone could keep all of those regulations, but, at least, their beliefs tell us about their love for the law.

The Sadducees were often at odds with the Pharisees. The ultra conservative Sadducees controlled the Temple and believed in the literal interpretation of the law. They would do whatever the law said, but that was all. They thought the law was diminished when you interpreted it.

The scribes, who started out almost as secretaries, were people who wrote. Over a period of time, they would copy the scrolls verbatim. Eventually, the people went to them, saying, "You have written the law. You did not create it, but you copied it and you know it so well. You have read every word of it. Since you have copied it time and time again, what do you think it means?" They began to be respected as interpreters of the law. The Pharisees had their scribes and the Sadducees had theirs, in much the same way we might have lawyers. They would argue with each other, back and forth.

When Jesus spoke to those two groups, would they hear him in the same way? Of course not. "What is your authority?" they asked. Jesus did not have the New Testament behind him. He could not look something up and quote it. The New Testament had not been written; the Christian church was not in existence, and Jesus was a Jew. "When you speak, what is your authority?" he was asked. "Our other rabbis speak, and they have the church and the Torah. What is your authority?"

We want proof to control; we want proof to manipulate; we want proof to be in power. Think of what we can do to other people when we know we are right. Do we not know that truth is an ongoing process? It is not just a position; it is a direction. "What is your authority?" "Know the truth," Jesus said, "and the truth will make you free." He was not quoting the Scripture; he was not hanging his answer on anything. "By what authority?" His reply cuts through our prejudices and our smallness.

A man who was enmeshed in the law came to Jesus one day and asked, "What is the greatest commandment?" Jesus knew that this man thought he knew and fully understood the greatest commandment. He was asking Jesus a question to check on Jesus. He knew Jesus could quote the commandment, but the man felt so secure.

At times, don't you feel ill at ease when someone comes to you, almost as a ploy, to ask a question when the person already knows the answer? You do not know the person is doing this, so you struggle, trying to explain something to the person. After a while, you realize that the person did not ask you to find out anything. He or she knew the answer all the time; it was just a put down. You feel foolish because you were struggling, trying be honest.

So it is in this case. The man came and asked, "What is the greatest commandment?" Jesus responded the way a classical rabbi would have responded: "You know it as well as I do; you know the Torah. What is the greatest commandment? Is it not to love the Lord your God with all your heart, mind, soul, and strength? And is not the second one likened to the first: to love your neighbor as you love yourself?" Then the man knew that he had Jesus, so he asked, "Who is my neighbor?" He was saying, "I want proof. I want to keep the commandments. Tell me specifically who is my neighbor."

In response, Jesus then told the parable of the good Samaritan. The hero in this parable is not a Hebrew; he is a Samaritan. This would be very much like telling some fundamental Christians a story in which the hero is a non-believer. How would that make them feel? The good person is not a converted Christian, not born again, not a convert. He is an agnostic, an atheist. Jesus told this story to the Hebrews. They could not take it, and neither can we.

Nonetheless, in this parable someone is beaten and left half dead. The people who see him are all "good," but they walk past him. They are not mean or bad. They are on their way to worship, and they ignore the person. One person, a Samaritan, stops and takes care of the man. He takes the injured man to a hotel and says, "If it costs any more, I will come back and pay that also." Jesus concluded the story by saying, "Now, who was neighborly? The one who helped."

When Jesus was asked, "By what authority do you do this?" He did not give any proof. He told a parable: "I have said the greatest thing is to love God and to love people. I have told you a story. So you are neighborly when you help the one who needs you. And someone is neighborly toward you when that person helps you when you are in need."

That is way beyond proof, is it not? There was no text to verify Jesus' answer—no tradition, no church, no authority except the kind of authority that really matters: the truth of the essence of reality. That is where we find God. That is where we find love and friendship. It seems to me these things are always ultimately beyond proof.

While we want assurance, we know so very much intuitively. We acquire a store of knowledge simply by growing up; a great territory of truth and awareness becomes ours during this process.

It is interesting that if we are in a crowd, so often we will feign ignorance. We will play down to the crowd. Fortunately, we know a lot more than we pretend to know collectively. I would have thought it would be the other way around. I would have thought we would act smarter collectively. And we are able to accept a lot more privately than we can pretend to collectively. Publicly, we are so shocked at things we already know privately.

Think of what we know intuitively. We have known intuitively for a long time that God does not prefer the Christian. We know God loves people. So we break out of our denomination; then we get out of our own little Protestantism; next we get out of the Christian faith and get with the Jews. Where do we stop? However hard we work to try to keep our prejudice intact, we have known for a long time that God does not prefer one race to another. We might prefer this, but we know God is not like that. Our own soul can outdistance the mores of the community. Intuitively we can go beyond what we seem to admit publicly. There is hope in that. We are better, sometimes, than we profess.

We do not like to be out on a limb by ourselves. We are all this way, which adds to the desire to be assured. We say, "God, give us some proof. If I cannot get it from you, God, I want to get it from my peer group. I need some group to reinforce me, to let me know I am all right and acceptable." Jesus faced that repeatedly when he was asked, "By what authority do you do this?"

Yes, we want assurance, but a relationship is what really matters in life, and that goes beyond proof. A relationship goes beyond a text; it goes beyond an act.

A relationship is what we long for. This is what the Hebrews wanted at the time of Isaiah. They said, "0 God, let us know." A relationship is what people wanted at the time of Jesus. They indicated this by saying, "Give us something that is identifiable. Is there not some sign?" And John the Baptist asked for proof, "Are you the one, or should we look for another? Where is the sign?"

Jesus said it so clearly: "Now, I have called you my friends." Can you imagine that, coming from the

Savior of the world? "You are not my servants. I am not going to batter you. I have called you my friends." Now, you do not have to know and be reassured, because you know one thing that is way beyond proof: You have a relationship of love with God.

7

The God Who Needs You

*A*n overview of the long history covered in the Bible introduces a powerful, mighty God, a God who commands respect and worship. We see God as always being in control; this God knows what he wants to do and will bring whatever he desires into existence.

When we read about the people whom we later think of as the Hebrews, at one point we find that they spent a long period of time wandering in the wilderness, because they could not bring themselves to move out by faith and take another land. Here again, the image of a mighty God predominates. The implication is that God is impatient and appears to punish them. They seem to be strong when they follow God and weak when they go against him. God's always being in charge is the obvious theme.

At last, these people decide they can capture Jericho. And the story reads, in effect, "It is given to you by God because God is God. God has selected you, and God is strong. God is in charge; God is in control." God's strength and power are recurring themes in both the Old and the New Testaments. We see a God we need, a God we fear.

However, the idea of a mighty God does not always make sense. For instance, we know that power tends to corrupt. If power corrupts us, what would keep it from corrupting God? If God is always power, how does God stay God in character, in goodness, in compassion, in love? Has that not crossed your mind? What would keep God from becoming demonic if God has all power and can do anything God wants to?

A baby is born. Now, look at the biblical story. The people living at that time did not know anything unusual was taking place. By and large, they realized the enormity of the event only through reflection. A baby was born. He could not take care of himself, so he was cared for by his parents and those who loved him. He was placed in a manger because there was no room in the inn. With all of his power, would you not have thought that God would have gotten himself into this world and been in charge? We thought that was the way God always acted. "But," someone may say, "God chose to do it differently." Well, if God has all power and chooses to do this differently, he is playing a silly little game. Is God pretending that he is embarrassed? Caught offguard? Is that the way God is? Where is God's integrity?

God is love; that is the plain truth of the matter. This theme is also in the Bible, and it is in reality.

Whether you believe in a compassionate God or not, that is the way God is. God is vulnerable, and God needs you because God is love, and that is the way love always is. So far as we know, Jesus never espoused the idea of believing in God's power as a way of righting wrongs. Jesus said, "Know the truth, and the truth will make you whole." Love is always vulnerable. Love has an honesty about it. Love can be strong; it can be firm and say what it thinks. Yet, at the very same time, love can be open and say, "I need you."

It is obvious that we believe in a God we need. Where would we be in our world, in our own mental, psychological, and spiritual journey, if we did not believe in such a God? A God who is; a God who will always be; a God we will never destroy, a God of love that can never be destroyed with all the hatred in the world because God is God. But God's character is presence, not the strong arm and the might.

Our problems around the world are literally manifold, which may be one of the reasons we want a God who is in control, an all-powerful God. This idea is promoted by television preachers time and time again. They say, in effect, "God can do anything God wants to do. God is in charge." I do not believe that. God is God, and God is better than being in charge. God is right. God is truth. God is love. And God is trying to get love to be in charge.

A gracious, lovely lady once told me about someone very dear to her who had suffered for quite a while before he died. No amount of medication made him comfortable. The pain he endured was unbearable for a long time. "Barry," the lady said, "there's nothing about that I can unravel or understand. If God is in charge and God can do anything he wants to do, why did God let him die?"

And then she told me a story: "I remember when he was a little boy. We were out in the country one day, and he found some scorpions. He picked them up and put them in a jar. He punched holes in the lid of the jar. He was bringing them back home, but on the way home, he asked me to stop the car. I asked him why, and he said that if he took them home, they would probably just die. So he wanted to let them out and let them live." And then she said, "That young boy was better to those scorpions than God was to him." "That's exactly right," I said, "if God is like you think he is. If God can do anything he wants to do and doesn't do it, then God's not very good, is he?"

However, God is not like that. God is like Jesus. Jesus was not able to do anything he wanted to do. But Jesus was the truth, and he was right. You can crucify him; you can kill him; you can do anything you want, but you cannot destroy him. This is true because integrity, love, and compassion, not power and control, are built into this universe by God. Whether we know it or not, God needs us. We know we need God; surely we know that. But we believe in a God and have a God who needs us.

We all need help, every last one of us. When we need help, we often turn to prayer. We are encouraged to pray, and we sometimes pray almost instinctively. However, the very nature of prayer suggests that we get what we need from God if we pray properly. The fact that we are having to ask God for it in the first place implies that God must have it, and we, quite obviously, know we do not. Hence, prayer suggests to us a God we need, but negates the idea that God needs us. However, the fact is that God is a God who needs us. That thought must be taught. If it is humanism, let it be. If it is Christian humanism or whatever else, don't get rid of it because you cannot accept the term.

The real truth of the matter is that one of the reasons you pray, one hopes, is to change yourself. For instance, if you pray for mercy, you might become a merciful person. If you pray for world peace, you might become a peace-loving person. Jesus encouraged us to pray to convince us to develop within ourselves the things that we are asking God for. By asking God for them and seeking them, we may find these things simply because we desire them. The reason we do not have them now is not that they are not available. It is because we do not want them and we do not seek them. This is similar to trying to give someone something that he or she does not want.

Prayer opens us up to the possibility of wanting the things that we say we are asking for. God, in this life, in this world, needs people who think as God wants them to think, which is exemplified in the way Jesus thought. That is what is so basically sound. When are we ever going to improve our world? The Dark Ages were dark, not because God made them so, but because ignorance made them so and blamed it on God. The people at that time were not allowed to think rationally, they could not ask questions. Certain things were taboo, and superstition abounded. The people did not grow, and they said their stultification was the will of God. Later, in the Renaissance, it was as if God were lifting the curtain so people could ask questions.

God has always been that catalyst, nudging us to

ask and seek. Jesus taught that repeatedly. I believe one of the things we need to stress is the fact that we have a God who needs us if we are ever going to make our world better. In order to make our world Letter, we must become a part of the human redemptive process. If we do not, we become more sophisticated in science and we are in the Dark Ages again without knowing it. We develop so much in terms of science, which is fine and can be very good, but science is somewhat neutral. It depends on how we use it. The humanities teach us the ways to use what we have. We need to help God redeem his world by becoming more humane ourselves.

One quality that may help us be a part of the human redemptive process is innate within us. There is something innate within us that encourages us to respond to someone in need. Have you noticed how many times the needs of people are mentioned when an offering is taken in church? I do not think this is done in an attempt to get your money. I think it is done for the same reason anyone would do it—that is where our minds and interests are. That is of importance to us; helping others is one of our priorities. However selfish we are, by and large, the desire to respond to someone in need is instinctively vital to us.

Chuck Yeager is considered by many to be one of the greatest pilots of all time. There are some fascinating reminiscences in his book, *Yeager: An Autobiography*, including one about Col. Yeager testing a plane over the desert. A friend of his was in another plane, and the two pushed the planes beyond what you would expect the planes to be able to do. That is how the planes were tested. A capacity had been calculated, and the pilots were to exceed that to try to determine the precise endurance of the planes.

As Yeager was flying, he realized that his friend in the other plane was passing out. He decided there was something wrong with the oxygen, considering their altitude. Yeager radioed his friend, trying to rouse him. He did everything he could, but his friend remained inert. Yeager thought, "Time is running out. He's going to black out at any moment." As a last resort, Yeager radioed that he was in trouble, that he couldn't make it. He said, "I can't make it," and then he went into a dive. His friend started following him. Yeager could not rouse his friend when he kept telling him, "You've got to come to." But it did something to his friend when Col. Yeager said, "I can't make it!"

How do you get to us? By bragging on us, by saying how strong and capable we are? We appreciate that, that is a part of the approach. Yet, there is something so positive about honesty. Was Yeager lying to his friend? Not really. What he had been saying all along was, "You need to come to, fellow, to save your life." Also, because he was a friend, he was saying, "I need you; you're my friend. You have a family, and they need you." That brought the man back to consciousness.

Sometimes you can become closer to someone in the awareness of a problem, in the honesty of a problem, than at any other time. Something within us instinctively wants to respond to another's need, which is where I think we really find each other.

One of the things that draws us to Jesus Christ as Lord and Savior is the fact that there was no place for his birth except a manger. Because of this we can think, "Someone with that kind of background can understand me. Someone like that can understand if I have a problem." And then you begin to think that you are not just dealing with Jesus; you are dealing with God. The story of Jesus' birth tells us that is the way God is. It is in openness that we begin to be closer to each other and to know each other.

From year to year I have participated in a profound service, held for the families who have lost loved ones through crime and violence. These families are the victims of violence. In a sense, the service is overwhelming to me. Hymns are sung, and different people make statements. We thank God for his presence and for giving us people to love. It is not a time to inflame passions, to make us hate those who killed our loved ones. Yet, those killings are inexcusable. Each year families gather and remember someone they loved more than life itself.

If you could, would you not like to dissolve all the pain and suffering of the world with your own sacrifice? We could find people by the hundreds of thousands, I would think, who would voluntarily say, "Do it to me, and then everyone else will never have to suffer like this." You would do that. You are not trying to be a Christlike figure, but you would say, "If I thought I could suffer one time and stop this demonic kind of destruction in our land, I would do that."

Jesus, I imagine, thought like that repeatedly: "O God, how do I stop them from doing to each other what they do? The war, the destruction, the anger, the hatred?" We do not know each other before we arrive at these annual memorial services; yet, we are a closeknit group because we are there for one profound purpose: Some people have been hurt beyond imagination; some people have been killed. Everyone who is there loves; we come together for that purpose, which is where you get to know God and where God finds you. This does not happen when your cup is brimful and running over; it happens when your cup is empty and dry. It does not happen when you have the answers; it happens when you may not even have a good question.

Throughout a long period of biblical history we know we have a God we need. God is like that. You need God, and you can turn to God any time you want to. God is always there. But, as is always true of any truth in life, we also believe we have a God who needs us. It is the way God is; it is the way life is developing. I do not know of a clearer illustration than when Jesus was born, the one who, it seems to me, shows us the nature of God. Think of what Mary and Joseph needed when he was born. They did not have a place for the baby to be born, except a manger in a stable.

8

The Intervention of God

*I*f you were asked, "Does God ever break into our lives?" you might very well say, "Of course, he does. There have been times when I've felt so close to God. When things were very good in my life, I felt an almost unbelievable exhilaration. And at other times, when nothing was going right, when I've been devastated by tragedy and thought my life had ended, when nothing had meaning, I have felt a strength that I don't know how to explain. I was strengthened and felt, by the grace of God, I can make it."

Your life will probably testify that God does intervene, but how does he do this? Does he interject himself and take charge? Does he make things happen?

Before we discuss these questions, we should

understand that much of our thinking is affected by what we might term a primitive approach to religion. Most of us are thankful, I suppose, for the stories in the Old and New Testaments and for the fact that they often show us something we need to see. However, just as frequently, the theology in these stories is very poor. This theology can be likened to our thinking as a child. As children, we did not think as adults think. We may have thought God was in his heaven right above us. We knew that our mothers and fathers, in most instances, could solve every problem. Things were black and white; we conducted our lives according to that credo.

Unfortunately, many adults demand that life still be that way. They insist God is right next door. God is the powerful, authoritarian parent who can take charge and make things happen. Everything is black or white in their way of thinking. At times, these adults have keen minds; yet, they are childlike from the standpoint of psychology, which means they are also childlike from the standpoint of theology.

For instance, the people who lived during the time of Moses believed everything that happened showed the power of God and was willed by God. Nothing could happen that was not in keeping with God's will, and everything that happened had to be of God. Good and evil were explained in the light of that reasoning. When something bad happened, God was teaching someone a lesson. When something good happened, it was because a person earned and merited it. If war was waged and lost, God had caused the outcome. But what had the vanquished done wrong? Then people prayed to find out what they had done wrong, and they corrected their mistakes. After this, they could kill those whom they saw as their enemies.

Today, to a great extent all across America, that is the way people imagine God. Regrettably, this erroneous idea is reinforced and compounded by much television preaching and teaching. From my point of view, when we reflect over a longer period of time, television preaching will be considered one of the most detrimental elements in our generation. These atrocious concepts of God could not be taught so successfully without a medium that catches people's attention and holds their interest. If these same ideas were voiced in a tent, many people would walk right by without listening. But television bestows on any concept an aura of respectability, whether it is warranted or not. That is true of all television preaching, including mine.

One of the erroneous concepts of God that we have allowed to flourish is based on our understanding of God. We judge God, by and large, by how we get along. Therefore, we do not let God be moral or ethical. We find this in the story of Moses. Moses died. Instead of his just dying because he was old, the people said God caused his death. They said God did not let Moses go into the land of milk and honey; that was Joshua's responsibility.

Now, Joshua was a child of his time. He knew how to fight, and he was devoted to his people. Almost anyone would have wanted Joshua for a military ally. But he was inept in terms of relating theology to humanitarian ideas or to society. So Joshua told his people, "This is what I want you to do. I want seven people to carry the ark of the covenant and seven to precede them with the rams' horns. Then all the rest will follow, and we will encircle the city of Jericho. We will do that for seven days and stand there being very quiet."

I would imagine the people in Jericho thought, "Those are peculiar people out there. Perhaps some kind of mystical seance is going on." And then Joshua said, "When we take the city, when God gives it to us, take the gold, silver, and brass and keep them. We will offer them to God. But kill every man, woman, and child." In other words, "Kill all the people, but God is going to give us the city." When the trumpets were sounded, Joshua's men charged toward the city, the wall came down, and they captured the city and killed the people.

That story is in the tradition of Hebrew teaching. Fortunately, many Hebrews read this account from a larger perspective, much better than so many Christians read it today. We can read it as being factual in detail and say, "That's exactly what God did because it is in the Bible. God did it, and those people were killed, which was the will of God." We do not ask, "What about the people living in Jericho? Did they not love their families? What is the real difference between the Hebrew army and the people in Jericho? They are all human beings. Do we not believe that all people are of God?" Of course we do. But we read this and play only one side of the record. We think, "If it's right for me, it must be right, O God, because I'm religious." When discussing this story, many rabbis raise the moral question, "What about the people who were killed?" This is similar to the Midrash's asking, "After the Hebrews cross the Red Sea and the Egyptians are killed, what did God do?"

The answer is "God wept, because God loved the Egyptians, too."

That is great theology, but, so often, that is not what you hear preached throughout America today. Instead, you hear the superficial, one-sided, prejudiced, myopic, blind type of faith that says, "O God, you are on my side, and we can zap any enemy." And this is done under the guise of following Christ. We have a primitive approach to religio:1, do we not? Think of the stories that are embellished; there is one about the sun standing still. According to the Scripture, Joshua needed more time to kill his enemies. God was concerned about Joshua, so God provided extra daylight for Joshua and his men to kill more people.

Several years ago when I said that did not happen, a lady wrote to me—she would probably flinch if she killed anything, even an insect—but her letter said, "I don't know how you can say that didn't happen. It's in the Bible. You know God did it." After reading her note, I thought, "Wouldn't it be nice if she let God be as she claims to be?" God did not stop the sun to help Joshua kill his enemies. People killed people. We understand that.

On the other hand, we are sometimes in danger of having a God who does nothing but intervene and do those atrocious, identifiable things. If you do not believe in a God who is going to come in and win for you by killing the enemy, what does the God you believe in do?

One of the reasons I think we have such poor theology is that it is so easy to remember; you do not have to think. You just have a little catechism of your own. You say, "I believe every word in the Bible." It is frustrating when you move to the other side and have to think. So we have two choices, and I reject both. On the one hand, we have a God who does everything, and on the other hand, a God who does nothing. God acts, of course. The question is how does God act?

God acts by being with us, not by intervention. God is with us; God has been with us. But when we experience or discover something, we almost think we created it. We think it did not exist before we found it, although intellectually we certainly know that is not true.

Think of a person who falls in love. That person may think that love was just waiting for him or her, that no one else has ever been in love before. At times, we have similar feelings when we are exposed to a new idea. Our enthusiasm and wonder make us want to tell someone that we have found something. We feel that it really did not exist before we found it; yet, we know it did. Some people respond to conversion this way. They have to tell someone about it, which is understandable, but it has been there all along. What happens is that we become aware.

God does not intervene in the sense of coming from the outside to the inside. But when we find the strength of God that can guide us through a difficult time or give us an insight that is admirable, beneficial, broad, or redeeming, we may feel that this strength did not exist until we found it. But the strength of God was within us all along; it has been released, uncovered.

God is within us, affecting us very much as leaven affects the whole. Jesus taught this idea. When you eat good bread, you don't boast about the yeast or other leavening agent that is there. You think of the texture of the bread. But obviously, you certainly notice when the leaven is not there. Quite often, the significant things in life do not call attention to themselves. The law of gravity works in a very quiet way. Oxygen is another example. The absence of oxygen or the threat of its being taken away frightens us. Many basics in life are just there, and we rejoice when we discover them.

Awareness, I think, comes from the capacity to be aware of the presence of God that is already within us. "The kingdom of God is within you" is the possibility of growth within us. This does not mean that all of God is within us, that we cannot find God in other experiences or that God is not out there somewhere. But the real strength in helping us to grow comes from within.

So God does not intervene in our lives in a direct sense. God is always there. At times we are fortunate enough to discover God's presence, and at other times we may think we have discovered it and call it God when we are being cruel or malicious. That is not God. It is never God unless it is compassionate, unless it has love.

When we think of the intervention of God, one mistake we make is believing we can drum up God. We think we can get God to act if we pray enough or if we are good enough. That is one reason why we will make all kinds of promises in times of trouble. Every last one of us can do this if we are frightened enough. We can say, "O God, I promise I'll do better if you give me another chance." I cannot criticize anyone for saying that. But when the crisis is over, we can realize, "I don't have to beg God. My guilt, my fear,

my smallness were making me beg God." God
understands that.

We should see that our attempts to drum up God
come out of fear, not from the broad picture of God. If
a child is lost, his or her parents will promise
anything to get their child back. I am on their side; I
would, too. We can say, "O God, I will be more faithful
to the church. I'll do whatever." We know perfectly
well that a child is not lost because someone has been
unfaithful to a church. However, we are trying to do
what we can in our helplessness. In these circumstances and others, we further develop the idea that
we can bring God into existence. But God is with us,
whether we feel his presence or not. When we pray
and become aware of God, we feel his presence as if it
had just come to us; yet, it has always been there. We
do not control God. God is not a valet who responds
when we are good enough to deserve it. God is with
us, regardless.

Years ago in City Temple in London, I heard Leslie
Weatherhead preach. He is someone I admire very
much. He served the congregation of City Temple
during World War II. The church was bombed many
times; I believe they had to move to over twenty
different locations. I am sure that I saw him as being
larger than life, but thank God he was who and what
he was. His writing and preaching left us a window
through which we can see God better.

On the Sunday night that I had the privilege of
hearing him preach, he told about visiting the family
of a man who had just been killed in an air raid. The
man's wife, who was in her twenties, was sitting on
the floor crying. Her head was in her mother-in-law's
lap; she was also crying. The young woman turned to

Dr. Weatherhead, not really in anger or belligerence, although both responses would have been understood, but just out of her pain, and asked, "Dr. Weatherhead, where is God now? What is God doing?" Dr. Weatherhead responded, "God is sitting there with you, helping to comfort you. God is in the hands of this woman who loves you. God is in her heart, expressing her love to you and in your heart, expressing your love to her. That is one of the things God is doing. God, right now, is using people to help people."

So it is. God does not intervene from "out there." God is already with us in everything we do. Sometimes we will know it, which will be significant. Many times we will not know it, but that will be consistent with the fact that God is with us.

God is also with us in our pasts, which we need. As we grow older, there may be times when we are more vulnerable than we were when we were younger. As we become more intelligent, more mature, as we learn to love more, we are more aware of people we have hurt. This can make us overly sentimental and rather ineffective. It can rob us of the powerful portion of our lives that gives us direction.

Have you made mistakes? Of course. Have you sinned? Of course. Have you hurt people? Of course. Have you always been as capable as people thought you were? No. Have you cheated, cut corners? You have probably done both. And now you are outgrowing that; you do not want to be that way, and you remember what you have done. Does God intervene and change the past? No, not at all. But God is with you, so you are able to see the past differently. You do not have to whitewash it; you do not have to lie or run from your past. You no longer fear it.

Perhaps your past is one of the reasons that you are now a good person. You don't want to be called good, but you are. You do so many beneficial things. Maybe you are a loving person now because you knew what it was to be unloving earlier. Could the past you do not like be the seasoning that helps you become a healthy person? God does not intervene to change the past. But God is with you, and he can help you remember the past in a different way.

What about the future? Actually, we do not have to move into the future to be inundated with the earthshaking realities of problems. World hunger is with us continuously. There are financial problems in this country; people are penniless. There are people who are unloved, or think they are, and lonely people abound.

We need not look to the future for problems; they are with us today. We can give the past to God, and we must give the present to him. But what about the future? We cannot turn it over to God; he will give it back to us. However, our future is with God, and the future God has in mind for us is good. God does not need to intervene, because God has never left us—and he will never leave us for one second in our lives.

9

Mystery and Reality

*O*ne of the many intriguing aspects of reading the Bible is discovering the way it can bring ideas together by the use of paradox, irony, and, sometimes, the unexpected. At one point in the Bible we read a story that tells about a baby being born and placed in a manger. A star shone. Some men had been watching the heavens for a long time, hoping to find a sign indicating God would redeem the people. Those who had studied the heavens thought, "Times are so bad, we cannot help ourselves. We need someone to come and save us."

We can feel the same way, especially when we are desperate. This can be the case if someone dear to us is sick, and we have tried everything in the world to help the person. This can also be our condition when we wrestle with a problem for a long time and feel it is about to overwhelm us. We think we need a miracle, and we say, "O God, I need something to save me!"

The stargazers in this story looked at the heavens one night and saw a star, indicating the birth of a child. They went to King Herod, saying, "We've seen a star, and we wonder where we should go." Herod was very powerful at that time. Power is strange for many reasons, in part, because fear is probably an inherent part of it. When we see someone who is powerful, we may think, "Look at the strength." Let us not kid ourselves, that person is standing on a stack of cards. A leader in South Africa enjoyed power, but he was frightened of little children. So was Herod; fear and power go hand in hand. And power corrupts. It makes you forget; it makes you unaware. Herod feared the birth of a child, thinking, "Someone may be born who will usurp my authority." Therefore, Herod said, "Tell me where the child is so I might come and worship him."

Two things are occurring at the same time in this narrative: A star shines, and Herod kills. There is the mystery: the star and the destruction. Both of these elements are in this story, just as they both are in life.

Now, the first element, mystery, fascinates us. We enjoy suspense. We like the thought of someone's keeping us in suspense. We can find tricks entertaining and amusing.

P. T. Barnum's life has interested me for quite some time. In actuality, Barnum did not buy a circus until he was in his sixties, although I once assumed he grew up owning circuses. He thoroughly enjoyed entertaining people; this was vital in his life. At different times in his circus career he lost money, went broke, and then got some money together again and put on another show. People paid him well to entertain them, sometimes mysteriously.

Blackstone was a great magician, whom I saw years ago. I was a teenager, and I remember how delighted I was to get a ticket for a seat near the front of the auditorium. I knew Blackstone's act was trickery, of course, but I also knew he was an artist. At one point in his performance, he was standing on the stage talking, and then he suddenly disappeared. I knew he was somewhere backstage, but he was not where I could see him. I certainly got my money's worth that night.

Houdini was, perhaps, the greatest magician of all times. He accomplished almost unbelievable feats. One of his most famous stunts was to have himself handcuffed, then bound with ropes and placed in a trunk, which was locked and submerged in water. Prior to this, Houdini would have prearranged a meeting with people at a certain place at a given time. He would escape from the submerged trunk and arrive at the meeting place on schedule. I have read that at one time a jail was built that was supposed to be escape proof. To prove this fact, Houdini was locked in the jail. He took a concealed instrument with him; the small tool resembled a pin. This was all he needed to open a lock. Guards stripped him at the jail, so he lost the instrument and had nothing whatsoever to work with. The officials even filed his fingernails so he could not use them. Houdini thought that for once in his life, in the glare of nationwide publicity, he was locked in a cell from which there was no way for him to escape. Then, quite accidentally, he touched the cell door, which they had forgotten to lock, and he walked out.

Now, religion, by its very essence, by its very nature, is closely associated with the mystical. We pray, which is mystical. Can we prove a great deal by our prayers? Some people say they can. They will show you all they get out of prayer. But I am speaking of the intangible, the idea. You cannot touch, weigh, or prove love, and there is something mystical about religion. That is true at its very heart.

In the liturgical realm, is anything more essential to the Christian faith than Holy Communion, the Eucharist? If we study the history of Holy Communion, we realize it has gone through a number of developments. We do not know precisely what took place, but in our mind's eye perhaps we can see a young man of Nazareth sitting with his disciples in Jerusalem. This was shortly before Jesus was crucified, and he was saying, in effect, "I know that you have kept the Passover for all of your adult life. As a matter of fact, you started keeping it as children. It is important to you. The unleavened bread that you take is to remind you that you leave in a hurry; you don't even have time to let it rise. The wine reminds you of life.

"Continue to keep the Passover, but when you do this, I want you to do it and remember me. Continue to observe this feast that is so important to you as Jews, but also remember that I share the service with you. I shared the meal with you." It is as if Jesus was giving them the gift of Holy Communion.

In the church, the idea developed that Holy Communion was the literal body and blood of Jesus. The thought is that a change takes place in the elements when a priest says the prayer over them. This is known as transubstantiation, the change in the substance. Later the thought was, "No, it's not the literal blood and body unless the person receiving it is aware of that." We have wrestled with these ideas.

Today, in the Protestant faith, the thought is that the bread stays bread and the wine stays wine or the grape juice stays grape juice, and the change is in the person. In religion we are so enmeshed with the mystery that when we deal with the reality, before we know it, we move out into the mystery that has some validity to it. Yet, if we are not careful, the very tendency to go into the mystery can also make us rather sick and neurotic.

Now, not only do power and fear go hand in hand as in Herod's case, but a devotion that develops out of fear is destructive as well. There are devoted people by the millions all across America; yet, so often our devotion stems from fear. We can think, "I'd better believe in God, or I'm going to be sent to hell and I'll burn. . . . I'd better believe in God. What is God trying to tell me? I'd better believe in God because God will end the world, and where will I be?" So frequently our devotion is born of fear, and that is sick.

God did not create his world to destroy it. God created his world to continue, for us to be alive. The good God in the creative process is so gentle that he shows himself in the form of a baby in Bethlehem. Despite this, when we deal with reality, we move into the realm of the mystery to the extent that we negate the marvelous reality with our desire to be devotional. Thus we corrupt our thinking out of fear. Perhaps we cannot see this reaction in ourselves, but we can see it in others.

For example, we can see thinking corrupted by fear

in the Old Testament story about the Hebrews transporting the Ark of the Covenant. The Hebrews believed the Ark of the Covenant contained the Holy of Holies and was the most sacred object in the world. They believed God was in the Ark of the Covenant more than he was anywhere else. We do not know what was actually in the Ark of the Covenant; perhaps it contained part of the Torah, which meant so much to the Hebrews. Nonetheless, to them God was there, personified, as much as God could ever be anywhere; therefore, only a priest could touch the Ark. They were transporting the Ark on a wagon, as a man who was not a priest walked by the side of the Ark. He was obviously awed, privileged to be there. He was not good enough to touch the Ark. And then the Ark started to slip off the wagon. There was no way the man could allow the Ark to fall to the earth. In his thinking, the Ark was God's presence, so the man reached out and righted the Ark; he did not let it fall. Then, realizing what he had done, he died.

The Scripture says, "God killed." God was not responsible for the man's death. But the Hebrews concluded that God killed the man because, in their minds, God caused everything that happened. Therefore, when something occurred, God must have done it. But they were wrong in their first premise— God did not cause whatever happened. God is always love. You see, sincere, radical, basic devotion stemming from fear is dangerous indeed.

In America and in the world, we need an understanding of the mystery and the awe that come out of enlightenment. We will never know every- thing. But if we could have total awareness, increased knowledge does not erase the awe in life; it ought to enhance it. The more you know about physics, the more the law of physics amazes you. The more you know about music, the more often you are enraptured by it. Does an increased knowledge of psychology eradicate the mystery? It should enhance it. But this comes out of enlightenment, not out of ignorance.

If we are not careful, we will develop a devotion born of fear and ignorance. We see the bizarre and the unusual masqueraded repeatedly on televised religious services. A few years ago, we could have marked off these exaggerated claims and said, "That's ridiculous!" But, since we see them on television, we can move over into this sick realm and say, "After all, it may be true."

If a storm is building up on the east coast, we can see a devoted man on our television screen who says, "I command you, storm, in the name of Jesus Christ, to leave the east coast." And the storm goes out to sea. If that man can do that, let him pray for some other things. The truth is the storm went somewhere else while the man was praying. These two events occurred. But to think the man's prayer caused the storm to veer is very much like a man's touching the Ark of the Covenant, realizing what he has done, and then dying.

Be enlightened. Think of the storms that rage and kill innocent people. When this happens, some other people may be praying. But God is not a valet who says, "I'll listen when some people pray correctly, but I won't when they don't. I'll be as mean as the devil, and I'll zap it to you if you don't pray right. But if someone else prays correctly, I'll listen." Do we have a capricious, small God who plays tricks on us in a mystical way?

We are open to the mystery, because we are intelligent people who are both fascinated and bored by reality. Regrettably, unless we temper our mystery with some form of enlightenment, we become superstitious, and our religion grows out of ignorance while we become more devoted. When Jesus said, "Know the truth, and the truth will make you free," he spoke to the mind. But at the same time, he also spoke to the heart. Jesus may be the only person who has ever had the proper balance between the mystical and the real.

To live a healthy life today, we need to find the appropriate balance between mystery and reality, and we need to have a sense of humor. This does not mean that we will always laugh. That would be absurd. Some things are so critical that laughter would be blasphemy. However, there is more to a sense of humor than laughter—a sense of humor provides a flexible way of being able to enjoy life. And, in this flexibility, we find a balance.

Unfortunately, people are often inclined to lose their sense of humor when they become radically religious. Yet, if you are healthy, there is a time when humor ought to be a part of your life. If you have not laughed lately, it is probably not because you are too religious. You may be dealing with some things that are closing the windows and bringing in darkness. It may be that you are living more out of fear than out of love. But there is a time when I think we need to have an awareness of a sense of humor. We need this in our lives.

And we also need a certain flexibility. In dealing

with who you are, occasionally sit down and read a book, think your own thoughts. You are the only one who is ever going to live the life you are living. What is the balance that you ought to have? On the one hand, a keen mind; on the other hand, an awe of existence. You know so much, and there are so many things you do not know. Your knowledge allows you to stand in awe and appreciate what you know and what you do not know.

It is also necessary that we be able to see hard, cold facts. We can decide that since faith is essential to religion, faith is healthy, and we should not doubt. But if we discard doubt and adhere only to faith, we rule out mental activity. Therefore, we tend to reject someone who seeks or asks the hard question. Over a period of time, we develop a creed that becomes fixed. It follows that the rest of our activities are to support the creed, without dealing with the idea that what we are saying may be wrong essentially.

In religion, I think it is healthy and redemptive when a person has both faith and doubts. Doubting is not bad; seeking and searching are necessary. If we need scripture to corroborate this, Jesus said, "Knock and it will be opened; seek and ye shall find." We ought to continue the seeking. One of the destructive things we do is assume we have arrived; hence we have our basic belief, and it is closed, fixed. Therefore, to us, anyone who questions our basic belief is wrong.

The truth of the matter is that balance is needed in a healthy person—a balance in religion, in politics, and in life itself. And the balance is always seen in terms of what we know, but we do not know it completely. We may be right in a number of areas, but we have not arrived. Therefore, the enemy is not simply some group that is against us or that we are against.

Not only should we see the hard, cold facts, but also it is necessary for religion to check on itself periodically by raising hard questions in reference to itself, rather than always defending itself with apologetics. American religion must do this if America is to be healthy. We are lying to ourselves when we continually act as if our group is always better, and we justify our elevated status by saying God selected us and we can prove this with the Bible. Healthy persons do not stop doing something only when they are compelled by law to stop. Healthy persons know self-discipline.

Therefore, we should not applaud blind faith and ridicule the questing mind. Both of these are essential; they are compatible as we look at the reality and mystery of life. Think of what we can see in reality that we know, which is sometimes a vantage point enabling us to see a vast area that we do not know. Yet, we are related to both the mystery and the reality. We can be awed by the reality that we experience, and we can be awed by the mystery in which we live daily.

As we acknowledge the necessity of insisting that hard questions be raised in religion, we should also realize that at times we must ask hard questions of ourselves. When we are working with a group of people, perhaps one of the best things we can do is speak against something that we hope the group will do. This strategy is employed not in an attempt to defeat the idea, but to work it out so it may have a chance for success, rather than trying to persuade everyone to agree with us at the beginning. But so often we work in just the opposite way—we do not raise the hard questions because we are afraid they might defeat what we want done. We do this in government, and we do it in the church, which is often detrimental.

Simply having the capacity to see what is, within itself, is probably an area of genius. When we look at our world, we realize that war breeds war; this goes on from one generation to another. When we view current conflicts, we see the people in other countries fighting one another. The two sides really are very much alike. The people are not motivated by disagreements in regard to communism or capitalism, although we think they are. They are simply trying to get through the day. They are trying to take care of their families and have a government that they want.

Yet, we want to attribute their differences to political philosophies. The reason you are living and doing what you are doing today in this country is not for any great philosophical reason. You are concerned about some very obvious issues—your job, your family, your friends, and paying your bills. So it is with persons in other countries; the great issues they are thinking about are the necessities of life.

In a healthy family, when children have a disagreement, the parents sit down and work with the children. How sick it would be if the parents were to equip the children with guns so they could have a better argument or a more dramatic disagreement. Yet, that is precisely what we are in danger of doing in terms of the world.

In the Third World, people who are uneducated, unsophisticated, and poverty stricken cannot be expected to act in a mature manner. You would not act maturely, and neither would I. Those people are going to fight to get their food and to survive. Surely we understand that. But in our country, with so many resources at our disposal, we make matters worse by playing the parent role and equipping these people with sophisticated weapons. Then, in their destitute condition, they can get at each other more effectively. We are the parent who arms the child with a gun. Is it not odd that we expect this child to create peace, that we expect the have-nots to create peace? They are incapable of doing this. Peace has to be created by the stronger countries of the world.

In order to reverse our flawed reasoning regarding other countries, we need to let our maturity catch up with our science and our sophistication. We need to go in as a peacemaker, rather than reacting and taking a side. These countries are going to continue to have conflicts; we would, too. We need to find a way to allow them to act as maturely as they wish. This will not come out of their poverty. They live in a crisis situation, which we aggravate repeatedly by arming them.

Reality, I think, can help to teach us a way to live with one another. But instead of seeing the truth of this, we treat it mystically, as if it is God's will that we continue living like this. We do not break the cycle. We allow the mystery to become ignorance and the reality to become inevitability.

We should deal with reality and also have an awareness of the mystical. The selfish can be changed so that they become generous. The cruel can be destroyed, not by bombs and bullets, but by a baby's being born and placed in a manger. That is reality. And, quite frankly, I think that is the biggest mystery of all.